CW00566498

FISHING FOR BASS

FISHING FOR BASS

Strategy and Confidence

Mike Thrussell

BLANDFORD

Blandford Press
An imprint of Cassell,
Artillery House, Artillery Row, London SW1P 1RT

First published 1989

Distributed in the United States by
Sterling Publishing Co. Inc
2 Park Avenue, New York, NY 10016

Distributed in Australia by
Capricorn Link (Australia) Pty Ltd
PO Box 665, Lane Cove, NSW 2066

Thrussell, Mike
Fishing for bass: strategy and confidence.
1. Great Britain. Fish: Bass. Angling — Manuals
I. Title
799.1′758

ISBN 0-7137-2051-4

Typeset by Graphicraft Typesetters Limited
Printed and bound in Great Britain by
Anchor Press Ltd, Tiptree, Essex

Contents

Preface
The Beginning

Few people are privileged to earn their living from a job that absorbs their minds and interests. For most, work is a compromise between the need to earn money and the satisfaction we may or may not receive from our job – and the first consideration weighs the more heavily. To survive, some of us devote ourselves to a hobby that serves as a release from the pressures of existence. I chose angling – or rather, angling chose me.

I was four years old when my father came back from work holding a book, *Mr Crabtree Goes Fishing*, or something in that vein. I have no idea why he bought it, for neither he nor I had at that time any inclination towards wetting a line, but that book heralded a turning point in my life. We lived in those days near the steel city of Sheffield, but on public holidays we made excursions to some part of the coast. The next such holiday saw the purchase of a cheap solid-glass rod, a suspect fixed-spool reel, and mussel for bait. My first cast, of ten or so metres into an estuary, produced a flounder. That single fish sealed my fate. Without it, I'm sure, my interest would have waned like that of any other normal four-year-old. More holidays were to pass before I caught another fish. My father's interest was never as intense as mine, though he never complained when he came along to keep me company; he came, I believe, more to enjoy each other's company than my – usually – unsuccessful trips. I am grateful to him for his companionship – and to my mother, who was often left alone when we had disappeared on a bassing or codding trip.

The ability to read has been the greatest asset in my life, for books allow us to absorb a lifetime's experience in just a few hours. So, to all the great fishing writers of my youth – Gammon, Brennan, the late Ian Gillespie, and more – thank you for what I now know to be such hard-earned knowledge so freely given.

If you can't actually be by the water with rod in hand, the next best thing is to talk about fishing with a like-minded person. Angling has brought me many friends: some I've fished with, some I've simply met, others I've just spoken to over the phone. To those I've fished with or met, I hope to do so again; to those I haven't seen, I hope to soon. My special thanks are due to Bob for his wisdom, encouragement, and the occasional verbal kick in the right direction.

My wife, Cori, no mean angler herself, often embarrasses me by landing huge fish when all I catch is a bootlace eel or pout. She puts up with my moods when I've lost a lunker, is (I think) pleased when all goes well, tolerates the lugworms and peeler crabs, and takes no notice when I wander in at 4 a.m. Thank you, love – for a townie you've done okay!

And, finally, to my five-year-old son, Mike – may it go full circle and I'll keep you company!

Mike Thrussell

1 The Bass

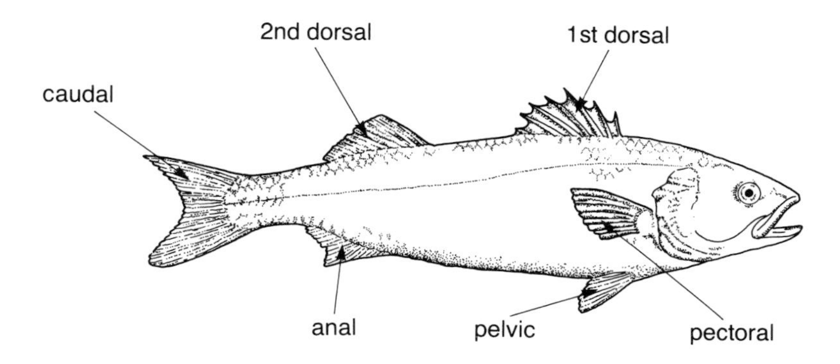

Fig. 1
Fin structure of bass

The European sea bass (*Dicentrarchus labrax*) has an immense following among anglers and commercial fishers alike. It has always been popular with the sporting fisher, but until recently the commercial fisher has taken little interest in it. Because of this, not much work on the biology and habits of this mainly inshore fish has ever been done. Much is still not understood today about this fish, although work undertaken during the last three decades has filled in much of our knowledge.

It's almost impossible to mistake a bass for anything else. It is a round, elongated, sleek fish having broad flanks covered in small scales. Its belly is white, shading upwards through silver flanks – often with a hint of gold or bronze – to a bluish–black or greenish–grey back. The head is bold, with powerful jaws and a cavernous mouth. There are no teeth as such – instead what feels like sandpaper gives excellent grip. The deep, dark eyes, with their gold-rimmed pupils, can move independently and are jointly capable of an almost 360° arc. The broad tail is capable of pushing the bass along rapidly in pursuit of baitfish. The lateral line is blackish and runs upward from the tail section to the head. Each gill cover carries a serrated edge on the preopercular bone and has at its base a razor-sharp point capable of ripping a bad gash across your hand. The large dorsal fin has either eight or nine spines (again capable of wounding the unwary) and a second dorsal runs towards, but not as far as the tail (see Fig. 1).

Bass are found from the Mediterranean up the coast of France almost as far as Norway, and around the coast of Britain roughly as far as

Fig. 2
Main area of distribution of bass

Northumberland in the east and the Scottish border in the west. Ireland has bass around most of its shores, although they are more plentiful in the south (see Fig. 2). Temperature has a great influence on the wanderings of bass. They penetrate further north in years when the previous winter's winds have had a mainly southerly push and have kept the Gulf Stream and its warming influence nearer the UK's shores. Winters with persistent easterly or northerly winds, which keep away the warming effects of the Gulf waters, are less good for bass. Bass based in the more northerly British waters overwinter in huge shoals in the English Channel and off south-western coasts, where the deeper water protects them from fluctuating temperatures. In mild winters they may stay around the south coast all through the winter.

Around March, when lengthening hours of daylight give longer periods of warming sunshine, the bass start their northerly migration. I believe that

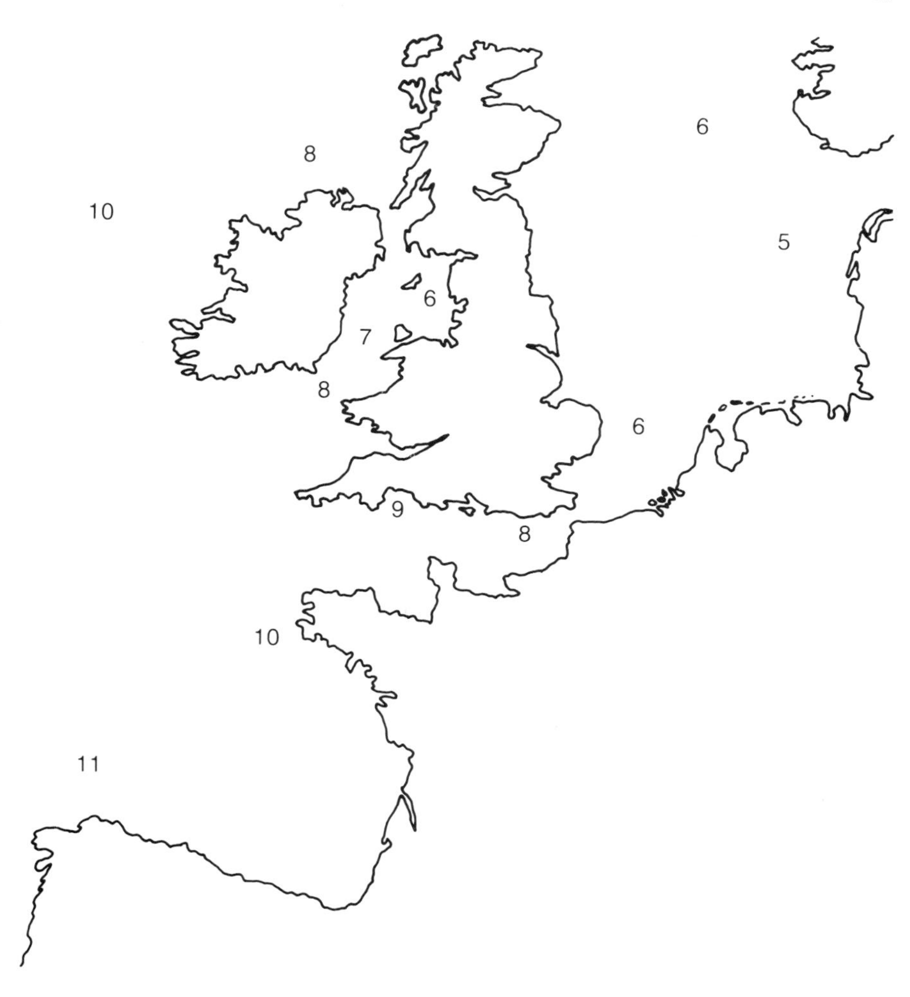

Fig. 3
Sea temperatures (°C) for March (mean monthly levels)

the bulk of the fish, when moving, stay in the deeper channels because of the steadier temperature there – the fish never seem to follow a course you can trace. For example, fish resident in the Irish Sea in summer cannot be traced as they are caught coming from Devon and Cornwall, through the Bristol Channel, and past mid-Wales towards Anglesey. The time lapse between the Devon fish showing and those of North Wales may only be two weeks. It's also interesting to note that the more northerly bass only show on beaches that give access to deep water. I'm sure the bass follow these deeper submarine avenues and slowly spread into the shallows as the water temperature rises.

Winter bass are usually caught in very mild winters from beaches with easy access to deep water. These fish are thin and in a poor condition and, while no evidence of parasites has been found, there is rarely any food present in the gut cavity.

Fig. 4
Sea temperatures (°C) for September (mean monthly levels)

For years, many anglers accepted the idea that bass begin to feed when the inshore water temperature reaches 10°C (50°F), but my own findings suggest otherwise. In the two areas I know best, inshore temperatures below 13°C (55°F) produce very few fish, even when bass have been present for a period of time. Nine years of careful obeservation convince me that bass are most active in water at a temperature of 16°C (61°F) and above. Noticeably, the peak numbers of bass occur in September when the sea's temperature is at its highest. (Remember that we are talking of the waters of the bass's inshore feeding grounds, where temperatures, unlike those of deep ocean waters, can fluctuate erratically – see Figs 3 and 4.)

School bass are particularly susceptible to temperature change. Low readings in the early part of the year mean that schoolies will be feeding hard on the bottom; a rise in temperature will see them rise off the floor a little way. By the end of May, with temperatures higher, adults will be feeding hard on the sea bed. As June gives way to July, they will be rising to take food in the upper layers. By early September, when cooling autumn winds rob the surface water of its heat, the bass begin their descent and again feed on the bottom. On those rare days of warm sun and no wind bass will be right on the surface, but the slightest wind will push them down (see Fig. 5).

Bass are capable of enduring high changes in salinity. In estuaries they can advance as far as, and sometimes a little further than, the saltwater wedge. In my own area of south Gwynedd I have, on numerous occasions, seen bass travel on a tide as far as Penmaenpool Bridge on the Mawddach and Glandyfi on the Dovey – and I have met sea-trout anglers who claim to have caught bass on the fly even higher. These fish seem to be feeding, but finding natural bait is a problem so far upstream. An eel (or half a one, to be precise) is satisfactory, but there is a long wait between bites. I have found lobworms to be useless. The small flounders that are often seen upstream in pure freshwater provide the odd fish. But spinning has given me the most success.

Bass generally spawn between March and June, though in a cool summer with unsettled weather I have caught gravid bass in late July. For spawning, bass favour areas of fast tide races around offshore reef systems or the mouths of estuaries, again near rubbly reefs, where fast-flowing water disperses the eggs far and wide, improving their chances of survival.

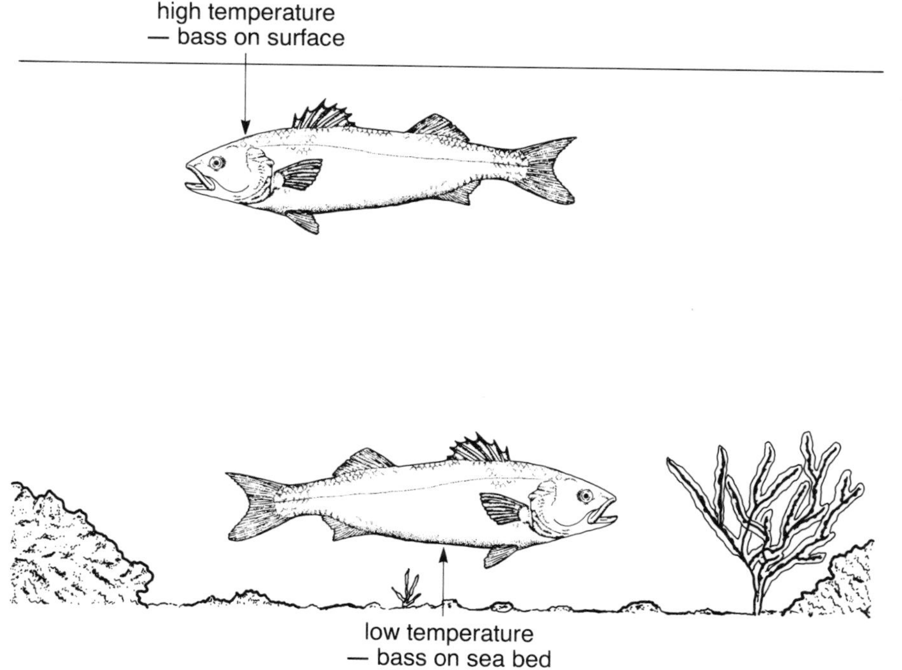

Fig. 5
Position of bass in high and low temperatures

The eggs are 1.15–1.50 mm (0.045–0.06 in) in diameter and incubation takes approximately four days. The prolarvae are 3.25–4.05 mm (0.13–0.16 in) long. They enter the estuaries and creeks when they have attained a length of around 10 mm (0.39 in), usually in July (though later in cool summers). By August they will have grown to 30 mm or 40 mm (1.17 or 1.56 in) and by late autumn to 50 mm or 60 mm (1.95 or 2.34 in), although this varies with locality. Their habitat is the small drainage channels and pools of salt marshes, which remain home to the juvenile fish for the first couple of years of their lives. They tend to use the deeper parts of the more main channels in winter and the bigger they grow the more they fall back into the main channel itself.

This reliance on the estuary environment lasts until the juveniles reach adulthood. The winters are passed in the deeper parts of the estuary or just offshore – you can often catch schoolies in the surf some distance away from the estuary in January. In shallow northern estuaries, fed by snow from the hills, captures later than November are rare. The deeper waters of the Menai Straits and the very wide and deep channels in major estuaries may hold juveniles right through the winter.

Females mature at five to eight years, at a minimum fork length of 35.5 cm (14 in); males at four to seven years, at a fork length of 31.5 cm (21½ in). The bass of one particular year form large shoals and stay together for most of the time until the onset of puberty. Often when fishing you get several bites first from fish of, say, 20 cm (11½ in) and then, after a brief pause, from fish of 35.5 cm (14 in). The two kinds never occur together and are always at different distances from the shore. These are school bass: two different year classes are running in front of you.

The small-fry seem to be able to stand very low temperatures for short periods, but prolonged freeze-ups prove fatal in the majority of cases. There is also some evidence to show that colder summers and winters have a marked effect on growth rates, although there may be an element of coincidence here. In the last forty years the 'good' years for bass have been 1949, 1959, and, to a certain extent, 1969; 'passable' years have been 1966, 1976, and 1979. This looks very much like a ten-year cycle, but I don't set too much store by this – for one thing, the spring and summer of 1986 were so bad that that year class suffered almost total annihilation.

Because bass are solitary fish, a female cannot guarantee when she may find an attendant male under suitable conditions, so spawning may take place on several separate occasions over a period of time. The eggs do not ripen all together and are not shed all at once. The males spawn only on one occasion. Female fish killed and examined in mid-spawning season often have half-filled gonads. Because of this 'on–off' behaviour the bass is never truly out of condition.

When the fish are young, males and females grow equally quickly, but with the coming of adulthood the female outstrips the male. Few twelve-year-old males weighing more than 2.25 kg (5 lb) are taken, whereas the female in British waters may reach and overall weight close to 13.6 kg (30 lb), although very few attain even half this. Mediterranean fish enjoy a much faster growth rate than those in colder climates, but they have a

1.4-kg (3-lb) bass taken on an artificial redgill eel, then returned

shorter life-span. Twenty-seven-year-old fish have been recorded, but any fish living to more than eighteen years is doing well.

In times of warm winters and summers, some movement of these southern bass into UK waters has been noted. These southern fish can be recognised by rapid growth rates in a relatively short life. Some areas seem to have a reputation for the consistent taking of slow-growth adults that are underweight compared to those of the same year class elsewhere. The reason for this – purely an assumption on my part – is that it could have something to do with food availability and the condition of the water. Repeating that these are purely my own thoughts, my findings indicate that a slow growth rate may be linked with areas of water that have a higher-than-average seal population. No parasites are evident on these fish – the only link is food predation by seals.

Bass have very few parasites, although a few years ago I caught a couple that had small intestinal wireworms. Nor do they seem disease prone. One I took in the summer of 1984 had a gill disorder that didn't seem to worry it; another had a spotted abdominal tract, but was otherwise healthy and quite fat.

Food patterns are fairly consistent, with few surprises over the years. The chief foods are shore and other crabs, and various fish – mainly sand-eels and fry followed by flatfish and others. Prawns and shrimps are commonly found filling the odd corner of the bass's stomach, but worms and the like are scarce – although this could be because the acidic juices of the stomach make short work of such soft, weak matter. Other food items, such as the occasional squid or small freshwater eel, are relatively unimportant. The juveniles feed on small plankton-like animals in the first few months, but gradually change to eating shrimps and prawns, then worms and small crabs.

By examining its stomach contents it's easy to see where a fish has been feeding. Crabs indicate rough ground, beaches, or estuaries; sand-eels, sandy beaches and estuary bars. Over the years you will recognise seasonal feeding patterns and realise when a change of bait is in order.

Adult bass become territorial, returning to the same venues year after year. They do not, however, necessarily stay near their spawning grounds – a bass spawned in a southern estuary or nursery is quite likely to take up residence as an adult in a location far to the north, or a northern-based juvenile may become a southern adult.

I'm not of the opinion that fish on a southerly migration keep to the same marine roads they used in the spring – for the further they go south the more stable the sea temperature becomes. It's also possible to ascertain the progression in the fish's migration through the captures you take as the fish head down coast, feeding as they go. This progression is also evident in the late burst of activity seen in some areas of Devon and Cornwall (and also Dorset) as the northern fish begin to drop back.

Bass probably don't feed at all in the winter, for they seem to make no growth. The likelihood is that they spend the winters concentrated in tight shoals, perhaps in deepish depressions, where they become semi-comatose, rarely moving, living on the accumulated fat from the previous summer's feeding. This fat can be seen when a later-summer fish is gutted – the inside upper edges of the stomach cavity have a build-up of yellow fat adhering almost the full length of the gut.

In an effort to gain more knowledge about the fish's movements, several campaigns of tagging have been undertaken and although recaptures have been low some interesting points have been noted. Bass are often recaught at the same mark from which they were tagged, giving confirmation to the theory that they are to some extent territorial and return to the same feeding grounds each summer. Occasionally, however, adult fish are retaken – within a month or two of release – hundreds of miles from their place of tagging.

Summer-tagged fish from western and northerly waters have shown up in winter off south Cornwall as they drop back for overwintering. It is important to tag juveniles and adolescents because the more knowledge we gain of their habits, the better equipped we shall be to protect them. It seems to me that juveniles, certainly in their first two years, stay in the estuary environment but fish in the third and fourth year of growth are capable of travelling far and wide. The most likely time of movement is the

Tagged bass ready for return

spring and summer. It seems that by late August, when these year classes are most abundant, they remain and overwinter close to the environment in which they find themselves. Any movement is short, into water where the temperature is consistent and even. In the winter, these fish will work the bars of estuaries and run the surf-line when a blow produces white water. However, having fished the coast of Wales for many years, I've found these fish disappear throughout February and March, returning only on the second set of spring tides in April. Little trawling is done in my area, otherwise it would be interesting to see if any of these turned up in catches during those two months – for they must move only a short way off and again, perhaps, become semi-comatose. I have, however, failed to find any evidence of this from contacts further afield.

2 Baits for Bass

When selecting a bass bait it pays to 'match the hatch' just as a trout fly-fisher would, for rarely will the 'chuck-and-chance-it' approach yield favourable results. Bass quarter a given piece of ground and associate certain food forms with the terrain. Some of these foods are available for only short periods of the 24-hour cycle, and to use these as bait when the fish do not expect them means failure. Bass learn that a food form is available only at certain places at a particular stage of the tide. This place becomes a regular stop on their feeding route but they do not linger after the food-form activity has ceased – they move on. This explains why an angler can fish for three hours without a bite, take three fish in consecutive casts, and then again have no bites.

In my own area of Wales lugworm is a mediocre bait. It gives fair catches of school bass, but produces only the occasional fish of 1.4 kg (3 lb), and very rarely indeed anything bigger. This can be explained by the fact that we have next to no lug on our beaches and the adult bass, not accustomed to finding lug, stick to their usual diet. The schoolies, on the other hand, being members of a highly competitive group, cannot afford to be choosy, otherwise they would starve. However, in areas where lug are prevalent, this bait can give excellent results. The more knowledge you gain of the habits and life-cycles of the creatures that form the bass's diet, the more success you will enjoy.

CRABS

Shore Crabs

Shore crabs are the bass's staple diet, and for two special periods in the season they feed on little else. This is the crab that so often adorns the inside of children's shrimping nets and is seen scuttling away when the stone under which it was hiding is disturbed. The shore crab has an outer non-living rigid skeleton that is its body's support and protective armour. It can grow only by shedding the old shell and forming a new one. It is at this stage that the crab is most vulnerable to a hunting fish and also most effective as an angling bait.

The new shell forms beneath the old one. When it is fully formed but still soft, the crab (known at these stages of its life as a 'peeler') sheds the old shell by taking in seawater and blowing itself up like a balloon. The old shell is forced off to reveal a crab that is very soft and watery in composition. These are what anglers call 'softies' or 'velvets'.

The soft outer shell begins to harden rapidly. The process takes about six days during the warmer months and up to two weeks at the season's start and end. Crabs with half-hardened shells are known as 'crispies' or 'leatherbacks'. At all three stages – as peeler, softie, or crispie – the crab is excellent bait, though the peeler has the edge because its body fluids are relatively undiluted whereas the softie has weakened its scent by taking in seawater.

Peelers need warmth, so it is rare to find any before mid-April. I always look for the air temperature to reach a steady 10°C (50°F) before my first collection trip of the season. Week by week the number of peelers increases until about the middle of May, when a huge explosion of peelers is evident. At this time the bass become pre-occupied with crabs as food. This bonanza lasts until the end of June, when a different feeding pattern takes over.

Peelers do not come into their own again until late August and into September. Being vulnerable at this stage, the crabs need somewhere to hide and they are far from choosy, making their homes under stones or weed, in cans and pipes, in holes in estuary banks or harbour walls – in fact, practically anywhere that provides cover.

In the early part of the season, when temperatures are only just favourable, pick the biggest tides and search only the low-water mark, especially in the mud surrounding rocks. Check large beds of free-floating accumulated weed piled up on estuary banks and in the corners of gullies. Don't waste time searching the mid- and upper-tidal zone as this is exposed to low temperatures at night, which won't encourage crabs to take up residence. Start working the upper-tidal zone from mid-May onwards.

How do you tell a peeler from a regular hardback? In the beginning the surest way is to break away the last segment of the rearmost walking leg. If it's a hardback the segment will come away, leaving white strands or sinew.

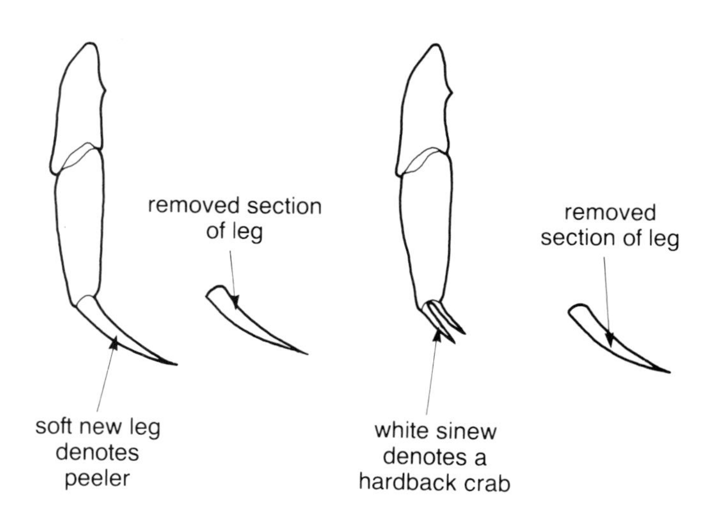

Fig. 6 Identifying peeler crab by leg-section removal

If it's a peeler you will reveal a perfectly formed, though soft, new leg section (see Fig. 6). Don't feel distressed at breaking away part of the crab's leg. When it's in trouble it's capable – at its own volition – of doing just that, thus releasing itself from its captor. Within a few hours it has sealed the wound and eventually regrows a new leg. Alternatively, look for a crack in the shell where the belly meets the back. The shell also becomes very brittle just before peeling. With more experience you can dispense with these tests because you come to recognise the state of the crab by its texture and colour: a peeler's upper shell feels soapy or grainy and the belly section takes on a dull, diffused colouring.

Crabs can only mate when the female is soft, although if the male comes across a suitable female while she's still at the peeling stage he'll carry her around underneath him until she peels and becomes soft. If the larger male is carrying the female with her belly down she is undoubtedly a peeler; if she is carried belly up she is a softie or a crispie. Pairing begins in May and continues until the end of September or early October.

To be a good crabber you need to be observant and meticulous in the way you search. Many people hunting through weed-covered rock miss as many as they find. It pays to lift weed up and away from its anchorage, looking in all the nooks and crannies and running your fingers under overhangs. Some crabs will sit in the weed, so check as you move it. Holes filled with mud and sand are favourite hiding places, so check at the base of rocks, where mud and sand is present. Run your fingers through this, as crabs like to submerge themselves completely. Places where loose, fine weed gathers, especially over soft mud, are also good spots.

Never ignore man-made structures or objects. Look around the bases of bridge or jetty supports, run your hands along the cracks of harbour walls, check the insides of tyres tied to mooring ropes and the weed that collects around mooring buoys that dry out at low tide. Run-off gullies in estuaries are enclosed between miniature sand banks and even these hold peelers and softies, though it pays to use a three-pronged weeding hoe to rake the sand as the poisonous weever also likes this environment. The steep muddy sides of estuary channels and tideways also yield crabs, though it's a messy business. If you walk along these run-offs, you'll notice deep holes like small rabbit burrows. These are crab warrens, the banks often being laced with a maze of interconnecting tunnels. The only way you can reap a harvest is to roll your sleeves up and plunge your arm in up to the elbow and feel around for the occupant – messy but very effective. It is possible to set trap lines to increase your productivity, though be careful where you place these so as not to endanger or upset people who need passage. Ordinary baked-bean tins are fine for this and are best placed, open end up, half buried in soft mud or sand at the average low-water mark. Old house tiles, bits of builder's piping, even staked-down fertiliser bags are also good, as are loose stones propped around the base of large boulders.

For a mark to yield regular supplies of bait it must be treated with respect. When you move a stone replace it exactly as you found it. If you don't, all life forms resident on that stone die and rot and no self-respecting crab will make a home there for the rest of the season. Make sure, too,

The author collecting peeler crabs

that you don't trap seaweed under rocks as this also rots and spoils the habitat. Don't rip chunks of weed from their anchorage. Replace crabs that prove useless for bait in ground already worked to avoid stepping on them. Working in this way you become familiar with the ground and learn every productive nook and cranny, so maximising your efficiency in bait gathering.

Having gathered your crabs, how do you keep them fresh? If you intend to use them within a few hours just add some damp seaweed to the bucket and leave it in a cool place. For longer periods you need a fridge, with the temperature held at no more than 50°C (40°F). Plastic ice-cream cartons make the best containers, but puncture the lids with several large holes as crabs need oxygen. Add damp seaweed, and keep the contents down to no more than twenty crabs. If possible, immerse the crabs in fresh seawater each day, but only for a couple of minutes, until the bubbles cease rising from their gills – otherwise they'll start to peel. At the same time freshen the weed and remove any casualties. Under these conditions peelers will keep for up to three weeks. Keeping the crabs at a low temperature delays the peeling process – the crabs become almost comatose.

Peelers, being highly scented, are most effective at times of rough, coloured seas when fish rely on their powers of smell to locate food. But, like softies, they are productive at most times and in most conditions. Presentation is important, but naturalness is not. A large bait oozing juices is far more effective than one designed for appearance. I start by killing the crab by pinching it between the eyes. Then I peel away the legs and shell to reveal a lump of meat, which I cut into halves or quarters, depending on the crab's size, with sharp scissors. I thread the pieces on to the hook and bind them with shearing elastic to form a juicy lump that is rarely refused. Make sure that the point of the hook is not masked by the bait, otherwise when you strike into a bite you will only bury the point further into the bait. Softies can be treated in much the same way, but whereas you can leave a piece of peeler on the hook for 15 to 20 minutes, a softie should be left on for no more than 10 minutes or so (see Fig. 7).

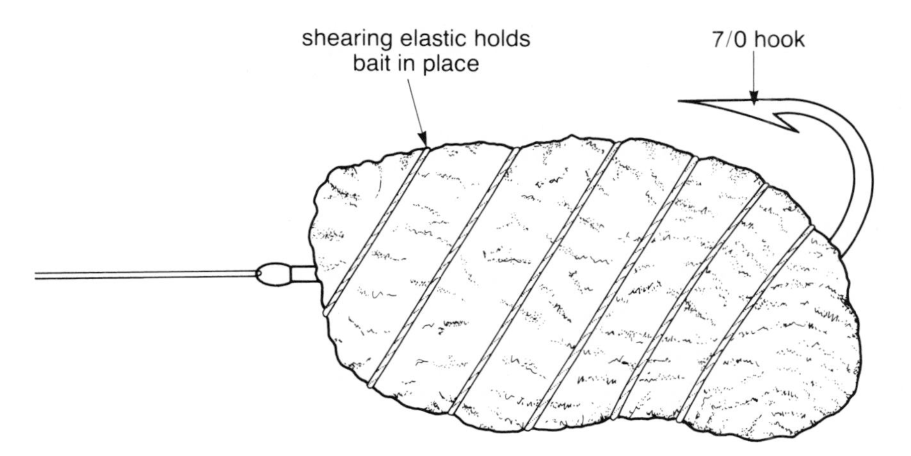

Fig. 7
Crab-bait presentation (actual size)

Edible Crabs

The edible crab is at home in deeper water and only available in numbers to anglers on the largest spring tides at low water. But it is a prime bait that often catches good fish when the shore crab fails, so, even though it is harder to collect than the shore crab, it is well worth the effort. There is no point in turning boulders and weed except at the low-tide mark. It is unlikely that you will reveal the whole crab, mostly only a small portion of the upper back will be visible. Gently scoop away the surrounding sand and with your forefinger and thumb lift the crab bodily from the rear – held in this way the crab's large and powerful claws will be unable to reach you. Most of the comments for shore crabs apply to the edible, but edibles only peel in any large numbers from July onwards. They are fairly plentiful in September.

The edible crab is fished commercially and its collection is legally restricted. Only crabs of a certain size, measured across the carapace, may be taken. So check the current ruling before you set out – the fine for taking undersized specimens may well be hefty.

The three main types of crab used for bait: top, the edible crab; middle, a velvet swimmer; bottom, the common shore crab

Quite large specimens are found in a peeling state and these may be cut into chunks in the same way as shore crabs. Edible peelers make excellent bait for deep, coloured water and fast tides, and are most effective if fished close to or on rough ground on a longish trace.

One other variety of crab is worth mentioning – though it is of interest mainly to anglers based in the south of the UK – and that is the velvet swimmer. This, like shore and edible crabs, inhabits rock pools and shallow reefs. Its eyes are a bright, fiery red and it is possessed of lightning reflexes, so watch your fingers. Neither edible crabs nor velvet swimmers keep well once consigned to the bait bucket. It helps to keep them in a container of fresh seawater with an aerator attached, but even this will preserve them only for a day or so.

Hermit Crabs

Hermits live in low-water tide pools in old whelk shells. One way of catching them is to bait a drop net with old mackerel and lower it to the sea bed from a harbour wall or groyne. Hermits haven't much scent and are not usually highly rated as bait for bass, but if you are fortunate enough to catch the odd peeler or softie, then that's another matter – mount several in a bunch and bind them with shearing elastic to make a sizeable bait. They are best used in calmish seas and on a long trace so that movement compensates for their low-scent value.

OTHER SHELLFISH

Prawns

Searching through rock pools at low water you may be lucky enough to find large prawns. These are good for daytime fishing, either on float tackle or ledgered on a long, light trace. In both cases the prawn should be hooked just behind the tail, a couple of segments from the end. Trotted down just above the sea bed they produce middling-sized fish. When ledgering, use the lightest lead you can and periodically twitch the bait back towards you a few centimetres at a time. You will find that the take comes during the twitch back, which simulates the natural evasive tactic the bass expects from the prawn.

Razorfish

Named after the old-fashioned cut-throat razor, whose shape it resembles, the razor inhabits the spring low-water mark of surf beaches. Several methods of collection exist, though none are particularly easy. The first, which some anglers swear by, involves using a spear of thin steel rod tipped by an arrowhead with two small barbs. This is inserted down the animal's burrow. When you feel the head enter a razor's shell you give the spear a twist to wedge the barbs broadside and pull the razor out. Or that is the theory. I've tried this method but I'm not over-impressed with it – often the burrow lies at an angle and on extraction it's difficult to follow the line, and the shell may break. A second method involves pouring a rock-salt or table-salt solution down the razor's burrow. The animal is thus led to believe that the tide is in and makes its way to the surface to feed, so that you can pick it up. This does work, but I find it far too slow for practical bait gathering.

The system I use is simpler. Armed with a stout, four-pronged potato fork, I walk slowly backwards along the low-water mark and look for the depressions in the sand that mark the burrows – they are in the shape of a keyhole. Sometimes a jet of water spurts up as the razor begins to bury deeper down the burrow, having felt the vibrations from your footsteps. Then I dig 15 to 20 cm (6 to 8 in) from the hole. You have to be quick, but with luck you will toss the razor out on to the sand. Sometimes, though, you will only uncover half the animal still embedded in its burrow. If it disappears, keep digging. If you have a chance to grab it, don't yank at the shell or you will just pull it off the animal. Hold the upper shell firmly and exert a slow upward pressure; you will feel the razor give little by little and in a few seconds you will have won your prize.

Razor is a good but not an outstanding bait. It produces well after storms, when large numbers have been washed into the surf, and makes a good cocktail – in some areas – when presented with lugworm. Feed the pointed head end up the full length of the hook shank so it lies straight. I leave a short stub of nylon on the hook knot, which helps to keep the razor in position during casting.

Butterfish

Butterfish keep the razor company on the lower tidal plains and are easily collected after a storm, when huge numbers are washed up. They show as humps in the sand. They make a fair bait for school bass but don't much interest the adults.

OTHER BAITS

Mussels

It may seem surprising to list mussel – and it is a bait I rarely use – but it can be a useful standby. Late in September, after an autumn gale, some good fish fall to it. Treat it as a peeler, using several to fill the hook and bind them together with shearing elastic. Bait size should be between a golf ball and a tennis ball. You can't make long casts because the bait won't stand it.

Clams

Clams inhabit the mudflats of estuaries and give their positions away by their tell-tale keyholes, which are bigger than the razors'. The clam lies 45 – 60 cm (18 – 24 in) down. Either dig down, following the burrow with a fork, or do as the best clam collectors do, get down on your hands and knees, roll up your sleeves, and put your arm in up to the elbow. Few anglers use this bait, but used whole and ledgered hard on the bottom in clearish water it sorts out good fish.

Lugworms

Lugs are rarely found on surf beaches where the sands are always shifting. They should be sought on sheltered beaches or in estuaries, on the mudflats away from the main flow that dry out as the tide recedes. The lugworm resides in the bottom of a U-shaped burrow, marked by a neat coil of sand and, sometimes, a small blow-hole. Dig between the two to reach the worm. When there is no blow-hole I find it best to dig 15 cm (6 in) away from the coil and at each forkful work backwards and deeper until the worm is uncovered. Sometimes you will see the worm half out of its hole. You can grab it and hang on until it gives way, as you did with the razor, but be gentle or you'll break it.

On more sheltered beaches you may find big black lugs or sewies. These burrow 60 cm (2 ft) or more deep, but the effort of reaching them is worth while because they make excellent bait. The low-water mark will hold the largest numbers and biggest specimens (see Fig. 8). The best extraction tool is a drainer's spade, which takes a narrow cut of sand and is easy on the back. Alternatively, on estuary mudflats where the beds are small but dense you can simply dig a trench, turning worms as you go. It's only ethics and sense to refill the holes as you go to avoid confrontation with harbour authorities rather than leave it to the tide to repair the scene.

Before storing lug, I always leave them in the bucket to cleanse them of ingested sand. Then I lay them out, about ten at a time, on a sheet of newspaper, making sure they don't touch each other, and roll the whole lot up into a parcel, which then goes into the fridge. They probably won't live like this for more than five days. Check daily for dead ones and remove them – they will quickly taint the others.

I like a bait length of about 20 cm (8 in), which means perhaps three worms with one fed on to the trace line above the hook. This is a good bait to use at night in rough seas, when these worms would naturally be washed out of the sand.

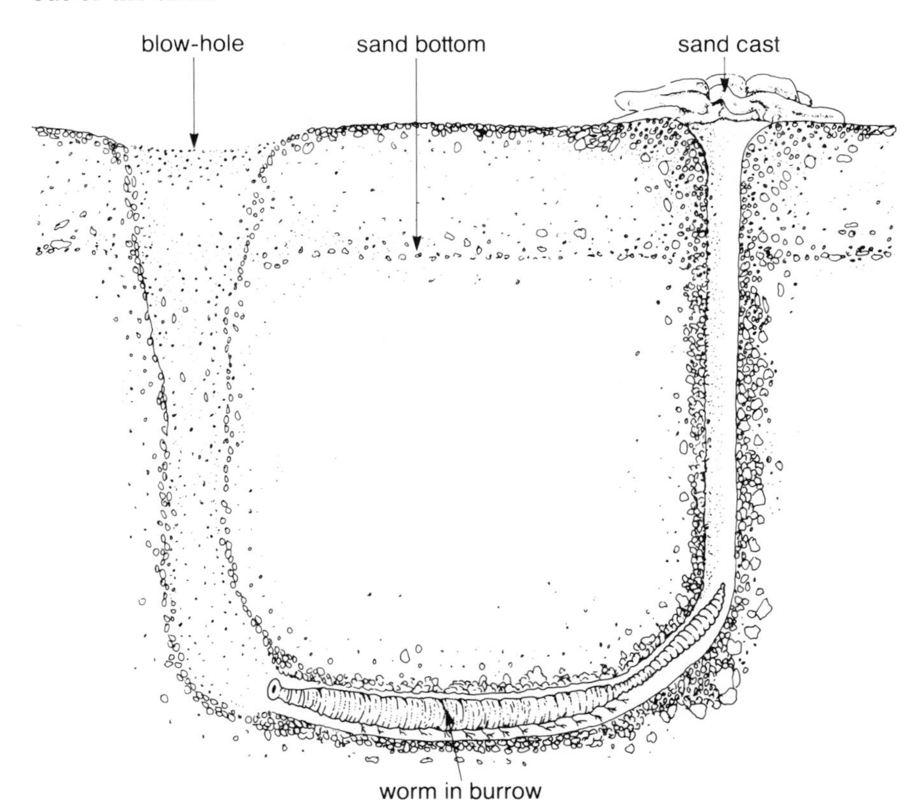

Fig. 8
Lugworm in burrow

Lugworms

Ragworms

You'll come across a few white ragworms (sometimes called snakes) when digging for lug in estuaries. These make fair bait – for school bass, not big fish – in calm, clear conditions when used on small hooks and left to wriggle. Keep the hook trace long and light. Whenever I've used king rag in an area where fish were feeding, I've caught. It is a confidence-inspiring bait, almost on a par with peeler. However, its extraction is another matter. King ragworms are found in the larger estuaries and on sheltered beaches; favourite places are areas of mud mixed with gravel and, occasionally, shingle beds and mussel banks. King rags are capable of reaching 76 cm (30 in) in length, though the average is much less. Their colouring varies from orangy–red and green to greeny–purple. They have two claspers at the head that often pinch the fingers of the unwary. Because they can show a remarkable turn of speed, fast digging is required. You find them by slow, observant walking, looking for their holes, which extrude a small amount of water. Dig in an ever-widening circle away from the hole, as the deep gravel allows, until you reveal your worms. Keep separate any that you cut or damage, otherwise they will poison the healthy ones.

Another method of collection calls for stealth. Creep up to a likely stone (usually a fairly large one) and if you turn it over you may find the worm caught unawares in its lair. Store the worms in newspaper in the same way as for lug, but pack them in fives or sixes, according to size.

King rags have a good scent value and make excellent bait for night or dirty-water fishing. They are useful, too, because you can add movement by leaving 5 cm (2 in) or so free to wriggle past the hook point. The bait size is the same as for lug.

FISH

Mackerel

The much-maligned mackerel is a bait worth having in July and August, when the mackerel shoals are very close inshore. A strip 10–13 cm (4 – 5 in) by 4 cm (1½ in) ledgered is a good form of presentation but, as large bass happily eat small joey mackerel whole, if you are looking for big bass free-line a whole mackerel or even half a one. To give added movement make a 'flapper' – cut two fillets up the mackerel's flanks, leaving them attached to the head, and remove the backbone, or just leave one flank of the mackerel in place. This bait gives plenty of eye-catching movement together with bags of scent, so it's good by day or night.

Pouting, Flounders, and Others

Pouting can be used like mackerel. A single fillet is effective, or their flank can be scored with a knife and they can be ledgered hard on the bottom. Small flounders make good bait for daylight fishing near the mouths of estuaries. Flounder is best fished on a long trace, so that the whole belly flashes as the tide rolls the bait over. The head and guts are good for the better fish.

Many other little fish are good bait. Blennies, small eels, and butterfish are best lip-hooked and fished live on float tackle. Whitebait, around in vast shoals during the summer, can be free-lined or fished on float tackle. Used live they are best hooked just behind the head to keep them looking natural.

Sand-eels

Sand-eels are excellent daylight bait when hooked through the top lip and fished live. Dead, even on a long trace, they are a second-rate but still not altogether useless bait.

Large shoals of sand-eels swim in estuaries and harbours and can easily be caught with a fine-mesh seine net. Not many of us, though, can use that method. We must search for them at the base of estuary sand banks that stay wet at low water, at the bars of estuary mouths, at the low-tide mark of surf beaches. The sand-eel lies buried in the sand at low water and can be found about 10 cm (4 in) down. At dusk it buries itself deep in the sand and stays there till dawn. Work a three-pronged hoe through the sand, but wear gloves – that flash of silver you grab for could easily be a weever. Sand-eels can bury themselves remarkably quickly, so fast reactions are the order of the day. Have the bucket and aerator handy, because they are difficult to keep alive.

Squid

Whole calamari squid up to 20 cm (8 in) long are good baits for big bass, having taken many fine specimens. Squid does have some scent, but it is a bait more suited to daylight fishing because its colouring aids visual location. Squid must be fresh. When buying them avoid any with a pinkish tinge to the body and trust to your nose – if it detects no nasty smells all is probably well. Squid is best presented on a two-hook pennel tackle, which gives good hooking ability and stops the squid collapsing into an unsightly ball.

Pushnets

Pushnets can be bought or made at home from any spare bits and pieces. They are simple to use. Given a fairly big tide and a gentle sea, push the net along in knee-deep or deeper water. Hang a bucket on your belt with a couple of centimetres of water in it to hold the catch, which, with luck, will include a host of small flatfish (remember size limits), sand-eels, shrimps, numerous crabs (even peelers and softies), and several varieties of small-fry. It's a good system and one to bear in mind when other bait sources are scarce.

Other baits will catch bass from time to time, but not consistently. The baits I have mentioned give at worst a fair chance of success if fished at the correct time and place. It's a waste of time and money to use poor bait. Personally, I have little time for frozen and preserved bait, which proves useless in my own experience. Learn to collect your own bait and to keep it fresh, and you're a long way down the road to achieving constant success.

3 Rough-Ground Fishing

Anglers who perfect a technique to exploit fully this form of bass fishing are few in number. The majority of anglers prefer to fish clean, sandy bottoms where there is not the constant worry of tackle loss. Yet this is where the fish are fewest – except to creatures able to burrow for safety, the flat sands offer little in the way of refuge. On the other hand, a beach covered by boulders, rocks, patches of shale, and thick beds of wrack and other weeds makes an ideal home for much marine life. For the bass, this rough ground is a pantry of plenty. It will always find some sustenance here. It may be distracted by sand-eel shoals in July and August or by mackerel hitting the beaches on a hot, still, high tide in mid-summer, but it will always return to the rough ground.

On the rough grounds the average fish is bigger than those taken from surf beaches and estuaries. Few fish weigh less than 1.4 kg (3 lb), fish of 1.4–2.7 kg (3–6 lb) are common, and a healthy number weigh in at over 3.2 kg (7 lb). Many people assume that deep water is necessary for good fishing over rough terrain – they expect to fish from cliff ledges many metres above the sea or rock platforms giving deep water close in. While it is true that deep-water areas, such as the Menai Straits in north Wales, can at times yield good returns, excellent fishing can be had also from marks where the depth at high water is only 1.5 or 1.8 m (5 or 6 ft). In fact, many bass reefs completely dry out at low water and fish the best when covered by only 60–90 cm (2–3 ft) of flooding tide.

Rough ground is a very loose term covering a variety of terrain. Not all of them are good fishing grounds – areas where vast boulders are scattered among patches of gravel are not desirable. Smaller boulders and rocks with clinging weed and growths are better food-holding areas. Shores of sand and rocky outcrops mixed equally are still productive.

It is essential to know the ground, and for this a walk at low tide is required when all the area you wish to fish is visible. You need to know where food is available to the bass, so you are looking for the nooks and crannies where the bass will hope to find a meal. Note how the stones and boulders are scattered, where holes and caves exist, look for overhangs and washed-out basins underneath rocks, see where weed camouflages rock pools and depressions (see Fig. 9). Look also for places to avoid – areas that

Fig. 9 Food-holding depression

have a blanket of what looks like coral growth are unlikely to give good catches because the entrances to the sanctuaries used by bass's food will be sealed off.

At low water the rocks may give on to clean sand or a mixture of rocks and sand, where marine life is prolific. Rocks may dominate, and food will still be plentiful as we reach the mid-tide point. At the high-tide mark the rough may give way to shingle and this last 23-m (25-yd) stretch will be almost barren of food forms. In deeper water, where the travel of the flooding and ebbing tide is less than on a shallow beach that may dry for several hundred yards, food will be found nearer to the limits of the rising tide.

It's important to explore the ground you are to fish – it teaches you so much of what a fish sees and experiences as it quarters the area. Turn stones over and you'll see myriad forms of life that depart post-haste as you flood their homes with alien daylight – shrimps, prawns, elvers, crabs, gobies, butterfish, and small wrasse. These are what the bass comes looking for and to catch it you must present a bait in the right place, at the right time, and in a manner to which it is accustomed.

The animals lurking in these rock pools and caves at low water come out to feed as the tide creeps over the shore. Watch how the incoming water seeks out the depressions, flowing in at one end and swirling around, picking up morsels of food and debris, and carrying them out of the pools and down channels between the rocks.

The significance of these channels only became clear to me when I began to understand how bass locate food. Originally, I thought vaguely of a fish either wandering through a maze of underwater obstructions in the hope of finding food by sight when a small shrimp or fish made a dash for cover or following the scent trail given off by an injured crab. I revised these ideas when I was able to watch, at close quarters in clear water, bass feeding among rough ground. I saw then that the bass faces the oncoming tide much as a trout does in a river, but, unlike the trout, the bass doesn't hold a set station for long periods. It lets the tide carry it a few metres backwards and sideways; if it makes a forward movement it is only to intercept food.

In this way it covers a great deal of ground while expending little energy. As food is collected the fish turns sideways to the current and allows itself to be swept some distance downtide until it finds another suitable vantage point. If you place your chosen bait into the depressions and rock pools, the juices are picked up and carried down the channels to the fish waiting below.

Food pushed in front of the tidal path tends to collect at the base of such structures as long, finger-like reefs, and the bass is quick to take advantage of this: at low water they approach these structures from the side the flooding tide is hitting. Drop-offs in the direct tidal path from shallow to deeper water can hold fish, but they tend to lie 20 or 30 m (20 or 30 yd) downtide of the over-fall. Any food washed over this spill falls forward and downwards, and this falling is anticipated by the fish. Use any deflection of the water to carry your bait's scent to the fish, and success will quickly follow.

Bass feed in these areas at peak times – usually low water, the first two hours of the flood, and an hour either side of high water, but fish can turn up at any hour of the flood or ebb. By finding out the peak times and only fishing these you will avoid much wasted effort.

Low water sees all the rough-ground inhabitants feeding, but during the middle hours of the flood, when the push of water is at its strongest, many food forms go to ground, being unable to cope with swimming in the increasing tidal pressure. High tide is another period of little tidal shift when many creatures are active. So low and high waters are both good times for the feeding bass.

You can set your watch by the arrival of the bass. A typical programme might be as follows: for the first 40 minutes of the new flood, you've a chance of fish at mark A: then, to keep in contact with the bass, a move to mark B is called for; here you've just time for three or four casts before the advancing water calls for a dignified retreat. No further action can be expected until 95 minutes before high tide, when at mark C fish will be resident for 25 minutes; staying at mark C gives you a chance of more fish 30 minutes before high water and 50 minutes after; sport then ceases. To some this may seem far-fetched, but what happens, I think, is that the fish respond to how the tide scours out a particular piece of beach – the peak times are those when the bulk of the food is being displaced.

Try to organise your trips so that high or low water coincide with dawn or dusk. It is when the light begins to creep over the towering cliffs behind you, but the quickening tide is oily black, that your chances of a result are high. Dusk and its fading light is equally good.

Many anglers say the spring tides give the best results, but, while I acknowledge that individual areas have individual characteristics, I can't wholly agree. Neap tides, when the flood of water is least strong, are worth fishing only at low tide, when the ground that usually dries out on the bigger tides remains flooded. You'll normally catch fish in the middle size range, though if there is a great deal of sand at this level the chances increase of hooking juvenile bass weighing over 900 g (2 lb). At the full height of these neap tides the water depth is often less than 1 m (3 ft) and although a bass at times is willing to feed in water that just covers its back, if the water is relatively clear it prefers to remain near the low-tide mark, where the extra depth makes it feel more secure. The biggest tides of the monthly cycles are those most likely to produce larger fish, up to a ceiling weight of 2.75 kg (6 lb) or so, but success is very hit and miss.

So neither the neap tides nor the big spring tides are the best times to catch bass. The water flow during neap tides is too weak to displace enough food forms to attract the fish. The push of a big spring tide is too violent for shrimps and small fish to be out and about and a hunting bass would have to use up too much energy for too little an edible reward.

There is, however, a definite link between bigger fish – of 2.75 kg (6 lb) and up – and the middle-size tides – 8–9 m (26–29 ft) on the Liverpool Scale. This is because all the factors are in favour of the bass finding a meal – the pressure of the tide is just right to disturb enough food forms to encourage the bass to feed without having to work too hard for a result.

But don't be put off by all this. If you have bait and wish to fish, then do so. Bass can, and will, show on pretty well any tide. It's never hopeless. I prefer though, to fish hard for short periods when I know the bass are there and feeding.

Pay particular attention to sea conditions. Often bass frequent a beach only when the wind is in one quarter, or perhaps two. When the wind is Force 2 to 4 off the sea and straight at the beach is a good time to try. So it is when there is a slight side wind. Both conditions help to persuade some surf to form, dislodging food secreted in the stones and lifting fine grains of sand and sediment into suspension and thus colouring the water – always good conditions for bass. Small amounts of seaweed are an encouraging sign, suggesting some agitation of water at sea-bed level. Some reef and rock marks are fished best during Force 6 or 7 winds and heavy surf.

A wind from the land that flattens the sea on the whole spells poor fortune. Neap tides, land-borne winds, and clear seas see few fish beached. There is always, though, the odd venue that proves you wrong. One place I fish does yield the occasional bass during periods of high pressure, easterly off-the-land winds, and constant sunshine with temperatures of over 27°C (80°F). You only get the one fish on the whole tide cycle. It can come at any time, ebb or flood. It is always big – weighing in at 2.75 kg (6 lb) or more. The reasons for this oddity are difficult to evaluate. I feel that the most likely explanation is that this fish is taking advantage of the fact that all the other fish are out at sea feeding on small baitfish shoals – behaving, in fact, more normally – and leaving the field clear for the maverick. Other beaches in other parts of the country produce these loners under similar daylight conditions. Daytime tides, though, are best avoided.

Freshwater rivers and streams that spill onto the beach can have both good and bad effects. At times of warm, still weather when the bass are lethargic and uninterested in food, the cooling effect of the infall of freshwater can induce a fish or two to feed. Fish at dusk and at low water. I aim to place the bait as near as I can to the junction of the mingling waters on the uptide side because it's here the bass will work. I haven't found them willing to feed amidst the main flow of the river proper, where the water is decidedly brackish, until 45 or 55 m (50 or 60 yd) downstream of the outfall.

During periods of prolonged rainfall, when the river water becomes filthy brown and turbid, the outfall area is far too acidic for the bass to be comfortable, and so it should be avoided (see Fig. 10). Walking the cliffs at just such a time I noticed how the brown rainwater was swept away by the flooding tide at right angles to the beach in question. This coloured water persisted though weakening all the time, for some 200–300 m (200–300 yd). The uptide side of an outfall, though coloured a greyish–green and full of suspended matter, is more likely to yield a catch. Remember this when the weather misbehaves.

Big bass and little bass don't seem to mix. If you hook and land small bass of, say, 1 kg (2 lb) or less, you'll not hook a larger one until the juniors have departed. There will be a period of 10 to 15 minutes before any bigger fish move in. Of course, the large fish may show first, to be replaced by smaller rank and file. Three categories exist: juveniles to roughly the 1-kg (2-lb) mark, youngish adults from 1 kg (2 lb) to 2.75 kg (6 lb), and then the adult group.

Reasons put forward for this apparent lack of socialising among the age groups are mostly theory based on logic: it seems reasonable that the small fish, being more agile, are faster to the food than the larger fish, who sensibly, therefore, avoid the competition. The adults are not averse to eating an occasional school bass in the region of 170–225 g (6–8 oz). It is rare but not unknown for a bigger bass to bully a smaller one away from an item of food. When I first saw this I wondered if the big bass was just a bit of a rogue, like an impatient shopper in a checkout queue, but perhaps it is part of their everyday behaviour.

Very big fish are to some extent territorial. They return to particular places at certain times of year and during certain types of weather. One fish returns to a corner of a beach I know every year within three days of 15

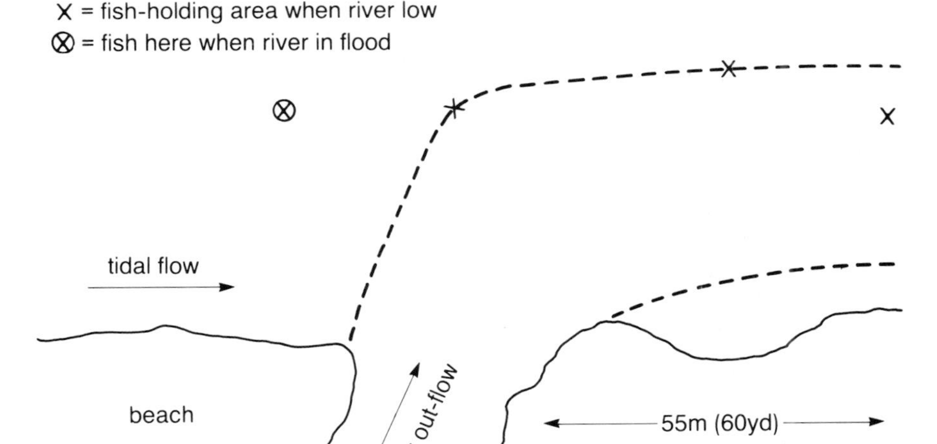

Fig. 10
River out-fall

May and remains there until the sand-eels take its interest around the beginning of July. I've watched this fish for a few seasons now and, of course, have tried to catch it, but it is wary of anything unless it's alive and swimming for it's life. It ambushes small fish as they are swept around a tide rip. Sitting high on a cliff ledge I sometimes see at low water a flash of its huge flank as it harasses the small flounders that fill a shallow gully. I look forward to this fish's spring return, although I know that one year soon my mid-May vigil will be in vain as it falls foul of another angler or natural causes put an end to the saga.

I've mentioned small fish, prawns, and shrimps, but there is one bait above all others that brings bass into the rocks to feed. That is the crab. Shore crabs, edible crabs, and velvet swimmers all have highs through the season and in different parts of the country. I like to start walking the area I fish about the beginning of April, but so much depends on the weather: if March is fairly mild and the first two weeks of April warmish, with plenty of sunshine on the bigger tides, it's then that the exposed rough ground begins to receive some heat. The water left in the rock pools gently warms up, as does the sea temperature – on the whole corresponding with the lengthening hours of daylight. This in turn induces the shore crab to begin to peel. Early specimens may be found as soon as the first week of April, but don't expect many until the third week. A bad winter and cold spring will delay this pattern by a further two to three weeks.

The bass seem to take 10 to 14 days to realise that the peelers are about, so the fishing hits full swing by the beginning of May and carries on through the peeling explosion in about the third week in May until early July, when the majority of bass move offshore to attack the baitfish shoals. Some fish return to the rocks in late August and linger on through September, feasting on edible crabs, which at this time are peeling in good numbers. Using this bait gives you the edge, but shore-crab peelers and softies will still catch fish. Save your best baits for when you most expect some action. It's often possible to pick your bait from the ground you are about to fish but, as most of the crabs will be towards the low-water mark, I dislike doing this. Invariably you are still frantically turning stones and hunting crabs when you should be fishing. I prefer to collect the crabs the previous day and so concentrate on the fishing.

When using peeler or softback crabs as bait, actual feeding areas can be small. You're back to those rock pools and depressions again. It's here where large, heavy chunks of food will lodge and, as we have already seen, the scent emanating from such places attracts the bass. While the tide is out, take note of where these holding areas are, and aim to cast your bait into one of these.

Productive ground lies underneath the rod tip at low water and casts of 18–36 m (20–40 yd) are adequate, even at high water. If you feel that bait is available to bass at a 9-m (10-yd) distance, then that's the place to fish. Casting further than 36 m (40 yd) increases the chances of your tackle finding a snag to get caught in and the angle of the line to the sinker is shallow, which means that when you lift the rod tip the weight is dragged across the sea bed, with the inevitable result. Hooked fish have more opportunities, too, to take the line around low-lying rocks and weed growth.

To prepare a crab for the hook, you must first pinch it between the eyes to kill it. Now carefully peel away all the hard shell from the belly and back, and remove the legs. You should be left with a lump of soft meat. I prefer to halve this with a sharp knife and then bind the two halves to the shank of the hook using shearing elastic. This creates a bait that oozes juices into the tide. Leaving the crab whole restricts the amount of body fluids given up to the water currents. Aim to create a bait the size of a golf ball, but more cylindrical in shape, and at all times keep this fresh by rebaiting at least every fifteen minutes.

On occasions it will be noted that the bass are picking the bait up but missing the hook. This behaviour is typical of the smaller school bass. To avoid this, prepare the bait as before but leave the legs fastened on one side. These are tied up the shank of the hook facing the eye, with the main meat disguising the bend of the hook – but not the point. This encourages the fish to take from the sharp end.

Deciphering bass bites is a conundrum of delights and frustrations. The sudden snatch on the line and the tightening of the rod as the hook finds a firm anchorage in the fish's jaw is pure bliss. The lunge seawards of the rod takes the unwary angler by surprise; the angler's hands flash backwards, lifting the rod to tighten the line. The weight of the fish is felt for a fleeting moment, then it's gone, and the angler is left only with a feeling of overpowering depression. I find it best, after casting out, to tighten the line gently but without moving the sinker. If you move the sinker, it's as like as not you'll drag it into a snag. Keep enough tension on the line so that you can just detect the feel of the weight on the rod tip.

A classic bass bite is the 'tap and thump', an initial, hardly discernible, tap followed by a savage thump with the rod tip being dragged seawards. Bass mostly hook themselves, and I find it best to let the weight of the fish set the bend in the rod. Ideally, this is enough to make sure the hook has found a bite.

Bass, having accepted a bait, turn into the current. If this turn is away from you – the angler – the bite conforms to the previous one described. If, however, the fish turns towards you and drags the sinker with it, you have what is known as a slack-line bite, with the line billowing in the wind. Invariably on rocks you can't run backwards, so you must rely on quick wits and a fast-retrieve reel.

Bigger fish – over that 2.75-kg (6-lb) barrier – are surprisingly gentle in taking a bait. If you get a faint tap but the usual thump doesn't follow, don't strike. The best ploy is to release a metre or so of line and be patient. After two minutes have elapsed, with no further interest evident, you may assume the fish has seen through your intentions and departed post-haste. But, after a long pause, you may feel a single, savage pull as the fish moves away with your offering. This final pull can be strong enough to unbalance the less-wary angler.

From time to time you'll feel the tension on the line drop and the sinker clatter across the stones. This is usually the result of tidal pressure on the line, but it could be caused by a fish that has picked up the bait and is rising in the water before making that turn away from you. Its actions are changing the pull on the sinker and lifting the weight from the sea floor. So, if you feel the lead move, strike – just in case.

Most unusual of all is a fish that, having accepted the bait, moves off in an uptide direction. The tension on the line stays the same and you get no early warning from the rod tip, but slowly you become aware that your line is moving uptide for no apparent reason. The mind usually takes a few seconds to come to terms with this phenomenon. Luckily, though, these bites are rarely missed.

How best to fight a fish? This comes only with experience, and you only gain experience by making mistakes. You have to formulate your own system of actions. My own, having made contact with a fish, is to bully them slightly to the surface. If there is a chance of the fish taking the line round a rock, I bully it upwards. I feel that to give line at this stage is courting disaster. The balance between holding a fish away from the rocks and ripping the hook out is a fine one. Let the fish fight the bend of the rod and set your reel clutch to yield line just past the point of the rod's usual fighting curve.

Bass, when hooked, tend to thump on the rod tip and thrash their tails on the surface, though this can also be because you are holding them too hard. Frequent jagged runs, taking 3 or 4 m (3 or 4 yd) of line each time, can be expected. Some fish sulk or pause for breath. Expect a sudden dash to the left or right, though the fish could swim straight for you, creating metres of slack line. If this happens, wind the reel as fast as you can, trying to retain contact. If tension drops and the hook has worn a hole in the bass's lip, lost tension means it could fall out.

Landing a bass is never a piece of cake. Some anglers prefer a long-handled landing net, which is fine if you can hook, fight, and land the fish from the same place. But what if it takes you walkabout? You need your left hand on the rod and your right hand to work the reel and there is no hand free for the net. Having played the fish to a standstill, I invariably gill it. Always pre-select a pool or area of flat sand within easy reach of the water where you can draw any hooked fish. Get into the water and, choosing a moment when the gills are flaring, shove your fingers deep inside. Beware the spines on the outer edge of the gill cover – they are as sharp as razors. Properly done, gilling gives the best grip on the fish. Catching hold of the open lower lip between thumb and forefinger, the thumb resting on the bass's tongue, is also good. Grabbing the wrist of the tail is less reliable – a good grip is hard to maintain when the fish writhes about.

Bringing a fish through the surf at high water or in rough weather is always a problem. You must use the incoming waves to deposit the fish on to the shingle and, in between waves, nip down and gill the fish. When a tired bass approaches the surf I back the clutch off my reel so that only slight pressure gives line back to it. If you have a situation where the bass lies half in and half out of the waves all won't be lost if you let the surf drag the fish bodily back, but if you try to hold it against the surf you've a good chance of losing it by the line parting or the hook pulling out.

Gilling a 2.5-kg ($5\frac{1}{2}$-lb) fish on a rough-ground bass beach

Even for this brutal ground I don't like to use tackle that is over-heavy. A light, fairly fast taper rod designed to cast 28–85 g (1–3 oz), coupled with a small fast-retrieve multiplier with or without the level-wind system, and filled with 6.8–8 kg (15–18 lb) breaking-strain line is often adequate. If, however, your chosen venue has huge rocks covered in barnacles and sharp edges and the tackle is to be brought over vast weed beds, then a reel in the ABU 7000 class loaded with line lested to 115 kg (25 lb) is a better choice. This larger reel may spoil the feel of the lighter rod, so match your tackle to the terrain. A fixed-spool reel is just as effective as a multiplier. The reason that multipliers are preferred by most rough-ground fishers is that once you're competent with them they are more satisfying to use and they give a direct feel when a fish is on.

The line need not be an expensive brand – the snarly ground can't tell the difference between cheap and dear – but don't go too cheap when using lines around 6.8-kg (15-lb) test. After each cast check the last 6 m (20 ft) and cut off any abraded line. Don't risk just one more cast – it may lose you a fish!

The running paternoster is the best terminal tackle. Place a small swivel by one eye to run freely on the main line and attach a second swivel direct to the main line. To this, tie a hook length around 15–23 cm (6–9 in) long, on line that needs to have a breaking strain 1.8 kg (4 lb) lighter than the reel line. To the free-running swivel tie 0.6–0.9 m (2–3 ft) of line roughly 3.6-kg (8-lb) breaking strain lighter than the main line; to this the weight is fastened. The short hook length helps to detect bites and avoids the worst of the snags. The long weight link makes the sinker stay ahead of even a large crab bait during a cast.

If the weight or hook becomes fast in the sea bed a good pull with the line wrapped around a jumper-protected arm will cause this light line to part and you will lose only a weight or hook. Rarely will the two swivels jam. Hooks with long shanks in size 4/0 to 7/0 are best as you can load these with bait. Sharpen all hooks before use and check the points after each retrieve.

Weights by definition need to be expendable. Spark plugs are popular, but don't attach them by the metal bar above the electrode. Loosen the screw cap at the opposite end and loop thick nylon line around the threads, so that it is held securely when the cap is tightened. Fixed like this, the plug will fly cleanly during the cast instead of tumbling in the air.

Plugs are fine for calmish conditions, but they are not heavy enough for rougher seas; tidal pressure on the line will lift them, sweeping your bait inshore. In these conditions some form of expendable grip lead is needed. A perfectly adequate one can be made from a roundish pebble from the beach of roughly 90 g (3 oz) in weight, knotted into a sleeve about 15 cm (6 in) long cut from the legs of a pair of nylon tights. The nylon catches in barnacles and rocks and holds fast even under heavy tidal pressure. Pebble-and-nylon leads are better than plugs because when a fish takes a bait it often jams a plug between two rocks and a good pull by the angler is needed to break the sinker from the line. With a pebble, steady pressure from a hooked fish or the angler's rod easily rips the nylon and releases the stone.

I don't carry huge amounts of gear and tackle. My rule is, if it won't go in

Playing a fish – hold the rod at all times and feel for fish

my pockets I don't take it. But I consider the following to be essential: a small plastic box to house spare hooks and swivels; a honing stone to keep hooks in tip-top condition; a bobbin of shearing elastic (black if possible); two spools of suitable mono-filament for hook and sinker lines; spark plugs and lengths of nylon sleeve (kept in my baitbox); a priest made from a length of dowel 4 cm (1½ in) in diameter hollowed out at one end and weighted with 90 or 110 g (3 or 4 oz) of lead; a clean cloth; a small pocket knife; and 90 cm (3 ft) of stout cord on which to string the catch.

Always be aware that it's easy to get cut off on the flooding tide. Think safety. When I fish on into darkness I use a headlamp, which means that my hands are free to perform any balancing acts while I negotiate an exit route. If there is a definite element of danger, a spare hand-torch makes sense. And it is always advisable to tell somebody trustworthy where you are and what time you expect to be home – broken legs are not choosy as to where they happen.

Wear drab clothes that blend with the background and break up your outline. Hide behind convenient rocks when fishing baits close to the shoreline, for bass have good eyesight. Don't be too eager to wade the shallows before casting, as you may disturb fish already feeding.

While your bait is being attacked by small-fry and crabs you won't catch bass, but when they disappear you can be sure that there is something bigger and better in the vicinity. Eels, rockling, and small wrasse are good at impersonating bass bites, but if you remain attentive and hold your rod at all times you soon come to tell the difference. Seals pop their heads above the water from time to time and derisory comments ensue: 'Won't catch fish today – not while he's around'. This is untrue. The seal is a better fisher than any of us can ever hope to be. It knows where the fish are, and by its presence is confirming your wise choice of venue. I always do well when a seal keeps me company.

4 Surf Fishing

TYPES OF SURF BEACH

You can categorise surf beaches into three types – full storm beaches, flash beaches, and lee beaches, though most beaches are a mix of two types and sometimes of all three.

Storm Beaches

The full storm beach faces the prevailing wind head on and is rarely devoid of some surf activity. Even during calm weather, with high barometric pressure and offshore winds, there may still be surf, caused by storms far out at sea creating ground swell especially if the beach faces the open Atlantic, for even the beaches on the west coast of Wales are in some way protected by the land mass of Ireland. To gain the most from beaches like these you must understand how the characteristics of the beach respond to different weather patterns. Taking the visible spring-tide low-water mark as our starting point, we find first hard, fine, rippled sand slashed by occasional shallow draining gullies and sometimes odd patches of rough ground, mostly of large pebbles. The beach rises at first at a shallow angle, but then steepens. Towards the high-tide mark the sand ends abruptly and a high, steep shelf of shingle thrown up by the surf's scouring action offers the tide some resistance. This shingle is often supported by high sand dunes. Sometimes, on gently-sloping beaches, there is no shingle bank. Due to this the power of the surf is subdued by the long, shallow beach, and sand gives way without interruption to sand dunes.

The advantage of these beaches for the angler is that most of the terrain will be uncovered at low tide, so that the angler can see how the fish will search the beach for food. I like to walk to some high ground from which the beach, or at least most of it, is visible, and take a few photographs that I can have enlarged to study at my leisure.

It is equally important to don your wellingtons or waders and walk as much of the total length of the beach as you can. Wade into the pools left by the tide, run your fingers through the sand, and see how many creatures you can find. On rougher areas, turn a few stones and you'll see small crabs, shrimps, seed mussels, and even small fish. Note any empty shells, because these give an indication of what lives below the low-water mark – likely candidates are razorfish and butterfish. Worms will be well below the low-water line, otherwise the surf would dislodge them on an almost daily basis. There, too, will be sand-eels.

By all means take a fork along and dig down when you see a blow-hole – possibly you will find a white rag or a shore crustacean. The best way to look for bait, though, is to visit the beach just after a hard storm. Then, by walking the tide line, you're likely to find numbers of live shellfish that have been forcibly removed from their homes by the scouring action of the storm-induced surf.

You cannot pay too much detailed attention when walking a new beach. A shallow beach with few, if any, obvious features needs careful research. Note any small depressions in the sand – even if they are only a metre or so across they will hold some food. Wash-ups, where all kinds of flotsam and jetsam collect, are good indicators of water currents that carry food morsels shorewards. So are connecting gullies between sand banks. If few of these features are evident aim to place the bait at the bottom of an offshore-facing sand bank. Bass tend to run here at low water (see Fig. 11), searching for sand-eels and for the flatfish that will collect here.

Other features such as sewer out-falls, old wooden jetty supports, and breakwaters are homes to small creatures and juvenile fish. Don't overlook a change in ground composition, say from sand to shingle or gravel. Bass often feed at just such places, whereas if the bait is placed only a metre or so away on clean sand it will evoke no interest. Small shellfish beds often hold feeding fish.

Bass will feed along the full length of the beach. So start fishing at that end of the beach where the flooding tide hits first. This area may fish well for two hours of the flood. Mid-tide is best fished halfway along the beach, where perhaps you have noticed a small eddy created where two currents meet. Full tide finds you at the other end of the beach and this may fish for the top four hours. Then reverse your route back to the original starting point – except when, as sometimes happens, the bass take a completely different route on the ebb to that they travelled on the flood.

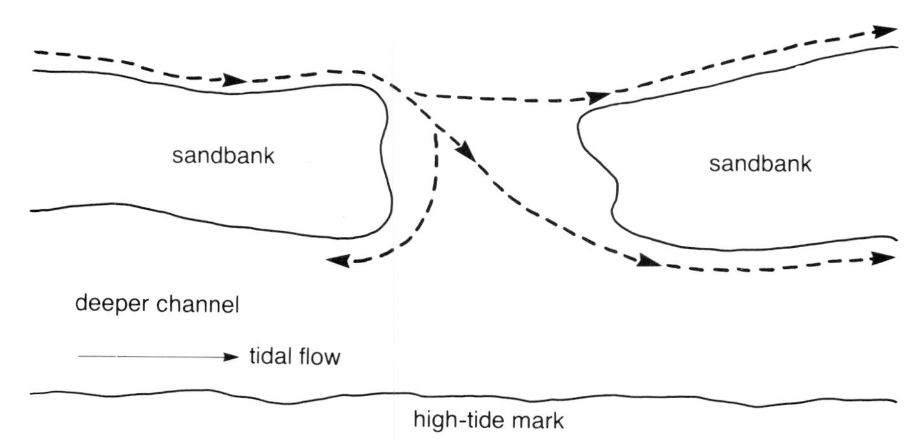

Fig. 11
Route of bass on shallow beach

Bass are hesitant to cross shallow sand banks not only in daylight but also in the dark. They prefer to stick on the seaward side where they are within easy reach of deeper and safer water. They do like places where freshwater streams flow out across the beach – even very small freshets of water or land-drainage out-falls hold a fascination for bass. Under spate conditions, though, the waters become too acidic for their liking and they will be found upstream of the coloured water.

Towards high tide note where surf penetrates a little further shorewards or where it is more turbulent, and try here. With the tide well up the shingle it's a good bet to place a bait at the very junction of that sand and shingle. Bass will be feeding here on creatures washed ashore by the tide and on the upper-shore life, such as sandhoppers, that have become available.

You can see from all this that bass visit an area only when they know that food will be available. They won't waste energy looking for food that isn't there. The angler must learn to recognise such times and fish only when food is available in good quantities to encourage bass inshore. It's essential to understand the rhythm of life that exists in a beach habitat.

A resident of such beaches is the common brown shrimp, which at low water is buried deep in the sand. With the onset of the first flood it leaves its burrow and swims off to feed. Two peaks of activity occur, at dawn and dusk. Shrimps are consistently active throughout the dark night hours. They are less active by day, depending upon the light – on overcast days expect some activity, on bright days very little.

Tidal plankton stays hidden under the sand by day but rises to the surface as night falls. Again, some activity can be expected when the water is coloured by recent storms and on dull days. You can read into this that night fishing is going to be most rewarding during periods of normal weather. True – but not at times of steady onshore gales, when all that food is being washed free and the seawater is thick with suspended matter offering little light penetration. At times such as these, bass will feed whatever the time of day or night.

I used to advocate fishing the tides that coincide with the cessation of the wind, but now I'm less inclined to agree with this (the ferocity of the storm must, however, to some extent be taken into consideration when deciding to fish). The former theory was that bass preferred to stay offshore during the height of the storm and to move in to feed when things had calmed down. My fishing results from this period were, however, at the best inconsistent. My thoughts about this were changed one day when I was walking a beach at just such a time after a storm, collecting live shellfish that had been stranded by the tide edge. All the shellfish I picked were whole and undamaged, though the area was also littered with empty shells. No damaged shells with the owners inside were found – even soft food like lugworms were always whole. Why should this be if the fish were only now beginning to feed? Obviously, seagulls were responsible for some of the empty shells, but what if the bass and other fish had actually been feeding when the gale was at its height, say at high water when the extra depth gave less agitation? Though the food source was at its most abundant, some

Heavy surf on a storm beach produced these bass, weighing between 1.6 and 3 kg ($3\frac{1}{2}$ and $6\frac{3}{4}$ lb)

shellfish must have been dashed on to rocks, thus being broken and giving the bass access to the meat. This can only happen when the scouring action is at its peak. The same goes for worms – some must be damaged when they're ripped from their holes, and they are easily found by the scent emanating from their wounds. When the storm subsides and the water is soupy, is it not possible that the whole worms we collect offer little, if any, scent, and cannot be seen due to the discoloration of the water? They thus escape being devoured – or is it that the fish are full and want no further food? Even huge surf is, surprisingly, fished with relatively light leads, and the former argument that bass are not powerful enough to swim in such surf is – in my opinion – incorrect. My findings show that bass will feed in rough conditions at the height of the storm, and at a state of the tide when water conditions suit their feeding. Admittedly, some surf is just too much, but this is rare. If you are fishing during the period of abatement the fish are satiated with food – at best they will be picky and at worst they will be elsewhere, undergoing a period of digestion. We, as humans, are the limiting factor, preferring to fish when conditions are kinder to *our* comfort, not giving consideration to the factors required by the fish we seek.

During these periods I've rarely done well using short casts. There seems to be some suggestion that a particular band of water at a given distance from the shore has just the right amount of scouring action to displace the shellfish. This band on a flood tide moves nearer to the shore, leaving in its wake its victims, which are – to some extent – left behind because of the laws of gravity. It's this quieter belt where the bass will feed. Ultimately, it's up to you to search the water to find this fish oasis. Weed after storms can also make fishing impossible, whereas at the height of a blow, the weed has often yet to appear.

Also worth bearing in mind is that the shallower beaches may be unfishable when the tide is at its highest and a huge surf surges high up the shingle or sand. Yet the same beach at low water can be quite comfortable, giving a solid but steady run of breakers that can be very productive. In more average conditions, results usually favour those who fish through the dusk and dark hours until dawn.

Bass sometimes work within a few metres of the shoreline. They can occasionally be seen swimming within a wave up to the beach and going back with it on its retreat. When a surf gets up after a period of calm, if you happen to be in the right place at the right time, you can see bass swimming in the clear waters at the top of a wave silhouetted against a bright sky. Why do they swim through the rollers in this way? It has been suggested that it is because they are lovers of oxygenated water and while I acknowledge that this is possible I feel it more likely that they are looking for food. When a bass swims through the crown of a wave as it runs up the beach it is, I think, using the roller as a lens through which to spy small fish and sand-eels that have been engulfed and swept along by it. This behaviour seems commonest at late evening when the low rays of the sun penetrate the waters and help the bass see better.

By full dark in calmish waters it often pays to ease down on the distance you are casting until you find the fish. On hot still nights, when bass are feeding in the surf, they may be within 4.5 m (5 yd) of dry sand and any bait cast 27 m (30 yd) will be totally ignored. A good trick to try at such a time is to free-line a whole pouting or mackerel deadbait that is lobbed out, say, 9 m (10 yd) and left to be swirled around by the waves. I prefer, when using this method, to slash the flanks of the bait so that it emits plenty of body juices. You can try this with a whole squid as well. Bites tend to be cautious at first, culminating in a headlong dash seawards taking several metres of line.

At night, simple orientation is required to recognise a specific location by familiarising yourself with certain landmarks. I like to pick, and if possible take a straight line from a static beach feature such as a particular sand dune or a small bush or large rock: something you can easily recognise in the dark. This helps you to find your rod rest and tackle, get your bearings dead right and you should be able to place a cast down the very edge of a rough patch on every cast.

In a surf with a reasonable run of tide, I use a grip lead of the type that releases its wires when it is given a firm pull. Most surf bites are fairly dramatic affairs – often the bass seizes the bait and dashes away. This gives the angler a start as the line goes instantaneously slack when the grip lead is freed. These fish are mostly self-hooking as they release the lead. Another classic bite is signalled by two bumps and a savage pull on the rod. When this happens I prefer to back up a few paces while winding the line tight – the increasing tension ensures that the hook has gone home. Slack-line bites, with the bass running fast towards the angler, are common. Again, walk backwards and maintain a tight line.

Bass fight with a series of lunges away from you, although a good fish that realises it's in trouble will make short runs parallel with the beach and turn its broad flank into the surf. Be prepared for a headlong rush seawards when the fish sees you and be extra vigilant if the fish allows itself to be brought in without protest for a few metres – this usually means that it is taking stock of the situation and brewing up its next move.

A big fish poses a problem when it is being brought through the last few breakers into the shallows. As its belly touches the sand its natural buoyancy – the buoyancy that lets us land big fish on light tackle – is lost. As the fish touches the sand its full weight is brought to bear on the line, which may break, and on the hook, which may tear free. Use the incoming rollers to carry the fish slowly towards you and when it bottoms out on fairly safe ground, follow the instructions for landing and gilling already given (see page 37).

Never haul the fish in by the trace and never use brute force with the rod to drag it ashore. You will be pulling against the dead weight of the fish and the trace may break or the hook tear free. None of this, of course, applies if you are fishing with a friend. Your companion can manoeuvre him or herself behind the fish and, using both hands, scoop it on to dry sand. I don't hold with kicking the fish to safety – you can easily tear the hook free and let the fish escape and, more importantly if the fish is to be returned, you can damage its internal organs.

Fishing a static bait is fine when conditions are rough but it's less effective in more moderate waters. For these I prefer to use a light lead with no fixed wires and let it be pushed slowly along by the tide. With a light rod you can feel the lead roll into gutters, bounce across shingle, and drop into holes and depressions. This system is ideal for searching fish out on those days when bites are hard to come by. If you let the lead have its head it will follow the natural water currents that carry food into natural traps. You can sense it travel across featureless sand and feel the bump as it falls into a hollow or gully. It's usually then that the bait is seized. If it isn't taken, you now feel the lead roll upwards a little as the line pressure carries the lead up the sloping side of the gully. Again, you can anticipate some action as it does so (see Fig. 12). Most of the common baits can be used, but bass expect to find sand-eels in this situation and it makes sense to bait up with sand-eel. If you choose a lead that is only just light enough to be moved by the tide and use a long trace, the sand-eel adopts what is to all intents and purposes a natural posture in its natural habitat.

Anglers are often disappointed at their lack of success when ledgering a static bait in a gully that channels a fairly fast flow of tidal current. The reason for the failure is that fish are to be found only at the exit or bottom end of the gully, where all the food impelled by the water collects. This situation rarely lasts for longer than two or three hours over the mid-tide period, when the tidal flow is at its strongest. If the exit to such a gully is stopped by a small sand bar then the bait should be cast about 3 m (10 ft) beyond this, where all the food is deposited and where the fish wait in ambush (see Fig. 13).

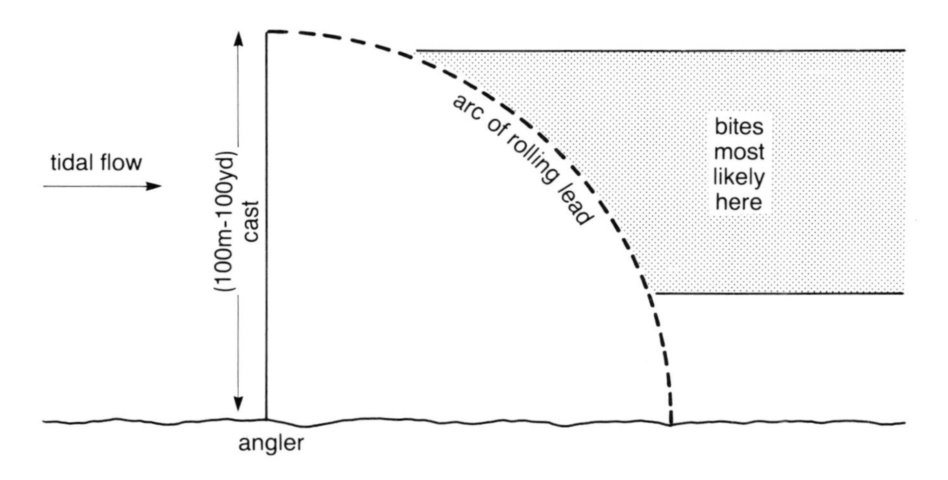

Fig. 12
Arc of rolling lead

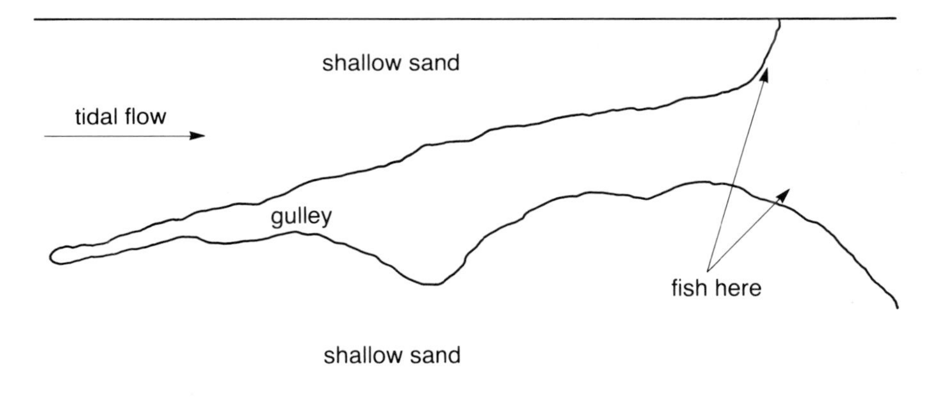

Fig. 13
Position of fish on shallow sand gulley

Flash Beaches

The flash beach has some of the characteristics of the full storm beach, but it is swept by the prevailing cross wind at a fairly sharp angle that stirs up a less ferocious surf. Flash beaches are likely to have a well-sheltered end where some marine life, such as lug, may hold a grip on a permanent basis. The sand is less hard and rippled than that found on the storm beach, though there is less likelihood of deep gullies and extensive feature areas, because the sand is not so often displaced during storms. Such beaches rarely match the storm beaches for catches of bass, though when the weather is moody and periods of gales sweep the shores the sheltered portion of a flash beach can be a good mark to try. On a storm beach, weed may make fishing impossible. There may be a wall of weed stretching the full length of the beach along the upper tide mark, with more in the surf and beyond.

The sheltered area of a flash beach is almost totally protected from the effects of the prevailing wind. As weed is carried not only by the tidal flow but also by the surface wind, the wind carries water-borne weed past this sheltered area, deposition only beginning where the wind blows onto the beach proper, leaving the sheltered portion weed free. Also, the water's agitation will be subdued here, giving better angling conditions. If the surf is really powerful, any fish present are likely to be feeding at the edge of the junction that lies between the quieter water (or eddy), and the current from the flowing tide and the wind's agitation (see Fig. 14).

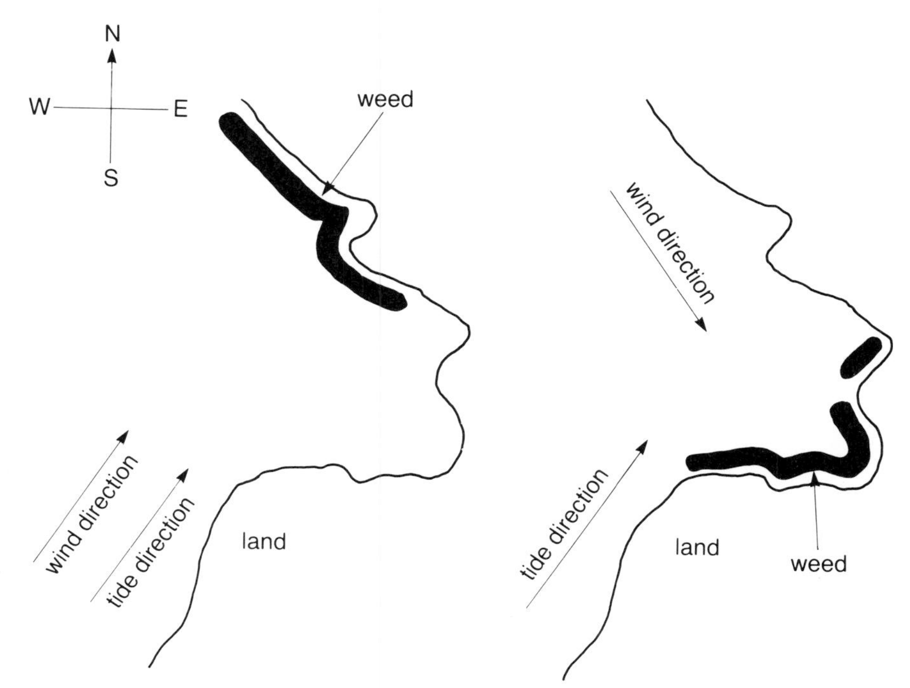

Fig. 14
Wind-blown weed deposits

If, for instance, this corner lay in a southerly part of the beach – with the tidal flow from the south west but with a wind of, say, Force 6 to 8 blowing from a north-westerly direction, the opposite would happen – all the floating weed on the surface would be pushed into this corner, leaving the rest of the beach fairly free.

If any pockets, however small, penetrate into the beach feature, these are also areas to collect weed and other debris on the side that faces the wind, and by fishing the lee side you may hit on to a small feeding zone just inside the lee point.

Under normal conditions, when fishing a flash beach, the features described for the storm beach will be equally important, but this time it's the upper end of the beach that receives those beneficial effects of the wind that give the angler the best results. Always look for surf movement in such places, or if none are evident, tidal flow. These currents can be observed from the shore by a line of rippled or lumpy water compared to the calm oily water at its side. Note also the floating weed lines. Hidden rocks and beds of boulders can often be detected by a patch of sea that looks different from its surrounding water – it having a slightly rippled effect.

As was noted with the full storm beach, the best wind for fishing is one that strikes the shore head on. This is true for almost every venue, and the same applies to the flash beach. This beach will only fish to its full potential when the wind quarters from a direction that strikes the beach full on. When this happens, accumulated food will be best displaced, and bass in good numbers are likely to take advantage of this. Any area of the beach that receives the wind – at any time – head on, is the best place to make your first cast, unless local knowledge tells you otherwise.

Lee Beaches

Lee beaches consist of very soft mud or sand (or often both), and contain a high population of marine life. One conclusion to draw from this would be that this high population should encourage large numbers of fish to feed. However, with an almost total lack of surf activity, no dislodging of food by wave action is noted, the food being spread evenly and there being no outstanding areas that might attract fish. Bass – if they are inclined to feed here – are mostly found at a good distance from the shore. They don't adopt a regular feeding pattern for a thinking angler to observe.

There is, however, one exception to this, and that is when a small river or stream has cut a path through the soft sand banks, and wound its way to the sea. This often occurs at the inner mouth of an estuary. Bass will often follow the flow of water as it is pushed back up this path by the rising tide, feeding on small sand-eels and crabs. However, as these beaches are shallow and drain quickly, the bass disappear rapidly once the first of the ebb gets underway. When you're lucky enough to get it right, a situation of this sort has the habit of turning up some extremely large fish – so it's worth some investigation.

The earliest you can expect to take a bass from the surf in the UK is in March, if the winter has been a particularly mild one. April is more usual.

Certainly by May there should be some good fish running the surf-line when conditions are right. They will remain through June until the beginning of July. After that and until the end of August, the fish prefer to shoal up offshore, and few will be found off the flash beaches.

The biggest fish appear when the first of the autumnal gales lash the coast. Then the bass return to the surf to feed up for the coming winter. By late October they are unlikely to be found except on the UK's southernmost beaches, though small school bass (mainly immature juveniles) stay in the surf until late January.

Most true bass anglers prefer to fish on their own, but if you have to fish in company there are certain things you can do to give yourself the edge. Your position in a line of anglers can be critical. If a line of anglers is fishing a beach and the flooding tide flows left to right, their combined casts will create a scent trail several metres wide, which hunting bass swim into and follow uptide. These fish are most likely to eat the first bait they come across, so the best fishing position is the downtide position on the furthest right of the line. The opposite end of the line is best, as the first of the ebb gets underway (see Fig. 15).

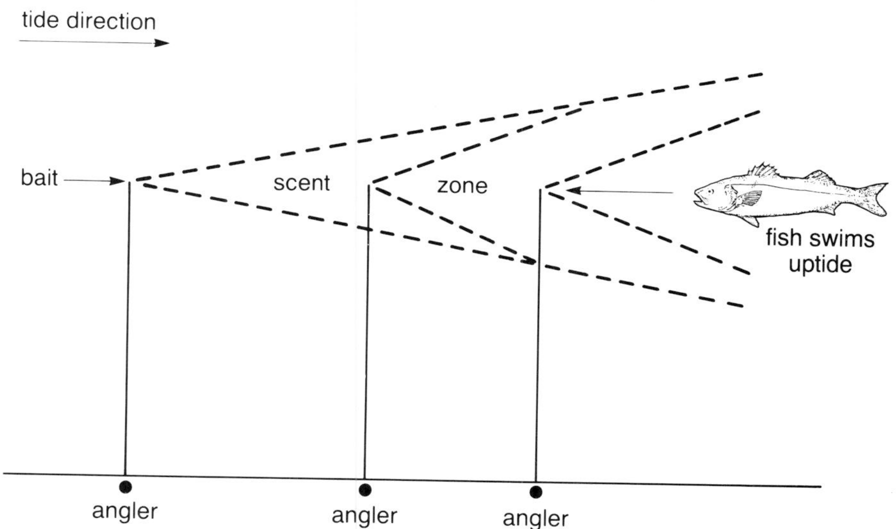

Fig. 15 Downtide position best when fishing in a group

If a large group of anglers are all fishing a relatively small section of beach and you are given little choice as to where you can fish – for instance, if you have to fish with numerous anglers to your left and right – then try to fish your bait in territory that is away from the competition of other anglers' baits and free from the constant bombardment of their leads. For instance, if the majority are casting between 60 and 70 m (65 and 80 yd) out and you have the ability to put a bait 110 m (120 yd) out, then put that bait out as far as you can. The chance of a single bait being eaten is good, whereas the chance of a fish eating your bait when it is bewildered by choice is limited.

This may work in reverse, because bass are often found within a few metres of the surf-line. Baits placed 75 m (80 yd) by other anglers may well be beyond the feeding fish. The right distance may be 18–27 m (20–30 yd), even if you are fishing alone. Though I normally advocate holding the rod at all times, the rule may be best broken on an unknown beach where, by fishing with two rods you can cast one out far and the other close in and slowly move them closer together until the feeding band is found. Even with just one rod, if bites are not quick to come you should inch the bait back slowly until you find some action.

Long-distance casting is rarely associated with bass fishing, but the ability to push a bait out to 120 m (130 yd) or more can be profitable. In certain situations bass may feed for a short period on a patch of gravel or on a sand bank out of reach of the majority of anglers. In rough weather, with heavy seas full of debris, suspended matter, and sand, bass will not venture within 90 m (100 yd) of dry sand, but a bait placed where the brown sand-filled water meets the clearer open sea (the line is always visible) could find bass only too eager to feed. All in all, time spent on improving your casting technique will be handsomely repaid.

Bass of different sizes no more feed together in the surf than they do over rough ground (see page 34). They invariably choose surf tables at different distances from the shore, with the smaller bass being closer in. If your furthest cast finds only juveniles it's likely that the bigger adults are out of range at 180 m (200 yd) or more.

In light surf I hold my rod out in front of me in a straight line with the line, and feel for bites with my fingers. In medium surf I prefer to hold the rod horizontally at waist level and at right angles to the sea, using a sweeping turn of the body to strike. By striking in this way you pull the line directly, eliminating much of the sag you get if you hold the rod higher and strike upwards. In poor conditions I hold the tip high to avoid the worst of the weed and on feeling a bite take the natural slack out of the line by winding it furiously and at the same time taking a few steps backwards.

Many anglers gain extra enjoyment from donning waterproofs and wading thigh-deep into surf. This certainly shortens the distance between angler and bait and thus makes it easier to detect a bite, but if you fish alone take great care – even a steady surf has hidden reserves of power that can sweep you off your feet. Then, with waterproofs or chest waders full of water, you could find yourself in difficulties.

5 Estuaries

Estuaries and bass go together like bread and butter. Estuaries attract the bass because they hold a plentiful supply of food, principally the shore crab. Bass also use the flooding tides that surge up the main channels of estuaries to carry them to the richer feeding grounds of the upper reaches, almost into the river system proper. One person could spend a lifetime fishing an estuary environment and still not learn all it had to offer. All estuaries are different, and all have their own unique characteristics. Some generalisations, though, can be made.

In the larger estuaries, such as those of the River Severn and Bristol Channel, you would expect to see areas of vast, shallow mudflats, numerous side creeks, lagoons that offer safe moorings for yachts, and, of course, the occassional lee beach. Heading out to the open sea, there are shallow banks cut by deep gullies carrying the strong tidal and river currents. These offer the bass excellent ground to satisfy their predatory instincts – mussel beds and rough ground, again exposed by fast tidal action. The land edges of these estuaries have either rough, snarly ground that is infested with weed growth and is excellent crab-hunting territory, or flat, muddy sand that inevitably claims the wellingtons and waders of the unwary. There are also rock platforms and small piers and jetties that give on to deep water, allowing access to even larger fish.

The outflow from major river systems is rarely, if ever, clear. Mostly it is full of suspended matter. Hence visibility is so reduced that the food-hunting bass has to rely upon its sense of smell. In these larger estuaries bass tend to stay close to the open sea and rarely travel into the narrowing estuary flanks proper. This may because of the mass of available food lying in wait on the ground previously described. No fish is going to travel any distance when food is close at hand.

Those fish that do make their way towards the brackish water will tend to stay to feed in the deeper narrow gullies that are scoured by the tidal and river run-off. Only on the very biggest spring tides, and then only at night, are they likely to wander from these deep sanctuaries to feed over the shallow mudflats. When fishing the deeper gullies it is unnecessary to cast into mid-channel, the fish will be found not there but where the highest concentrations of food have led them – at the foot of the channel banks, which are likely to be fairly steep. Use a long, flowing trace and a lead light enough for the tide to bounce so that your bait behaves in a natural manner.

On those big spring tides, any bass that thinks the open mudflats are worth investigation will favour areas of shellfish beds or worm concentrations. Ridges of shingle and shell where small baitfish congregate will also receive attention. But devote most of your time to fishing the odd rougher patch where crabs can be found. Crabs are capable of sustaining life for quite long periods away from the neap-tide line, providing they are in muddy burrows or under stones that never dry out. They become intensely active when the first new tide on an upward cycle reaches their burrows. The bass are aware of this and cash in while the going is good. Again, don't cast too far out. The fish may well be close in to dry land – in darkness they are happy in water that just covers their backs, even if the main dorsal fin protrudes shark-fashion from the water.

Surprisingly large fish are taken from the upper reaches of estuaries. Rarely do you see small school fish, possibly because of the distances to be travelled. In the upper reaches of a large estuary, fish are to be found for only a short period around high-water time, when the incoming sea has halted and repulsed the fresh water. Once the first of the ebb gets underway and the salt content begins to fall, any fish present will rapidly drop back with the retreating tide.

During times of heavy rainfall these larger estuaries reach high levels of acidity that may last for several days, until the run-off from the hills is complete. Fish will stay way out beyond this acid line until conditions improve.

While major estuaries deepen at their wide mouths as they meet the open sea and are laced with deep channels and high sand banks, smaller estuaries are rather different. The mouths of small estuaries are often crowned with a bar – an accumulation of sand, sediment, and silt brought down by the scouring action of the tides and deposited to form a natural barrier between the open sea and the estuary. This demarcation line is critical to the numbers of bass travelling the estuary. The sea side of the bar is frequently a steep shelf of sand that drops away rapidly to one or even two fathoms in a matter of a few metres. Shipping may only find safe passage over such ridges at high water. Usually there is a deeper, main run-off channel, with possibly smaller, shallower channels branching off it. At either side of these main run-offs, high solid fingers of sand form the flanks of the outer estuary. On the big spring tides these may dry out for several hundred metres, leaving water in the channel only. It's at these times that you can walk right out on to the bar proper. This sandy terrain may be the home of sand-eels, white rag, and perhaps a few hermit crabs. Over the bar into the main run-off channel there is a change from sand to shale and pebble, caused by the current from the out-flowing river constantly sifting the fine sand and mud away. Large expanses of seed-mussel beds are often seen, and the small reefs composed of washed-down river boulders may hold a few crabs. From here you can expect a change to a soft sea bed of muddy sand, especially if the channel widens a little. A narrowing of this channel, on the other hand, mostly denotes a change to a rougher bottom, as the tidal flow is condensed into a smaller space. The resultant increase in pace means extra depth may be evident, with a significant and rapid fall. Because of the funnelling effect of the tidal power, the channel may take a straight route for some distance, though sediment will build up on either side to create mud and sandflats – often extensive, and holding shellfish and worm beds. From here the currents lose much of their sting, and the channels become more snake-like, wandering here, there and everywhere. At the apex of corners, deep holes with exposed rock may be found – excellent food-holding areas. Finally, the upper estuary is composed of one, small, run-off channel, held in by high, muddy banks that lead on to spartina beds and saltmarsh.

The depth and composition of the bar is important to the bass's behaviour. If the bar is shallow, or dries out at low water, any fish wishing to run the estuary will shoal up on the sea side of the bar and cross over into the estuary only when the tide has flooded to a good depth. This may leave only, say, the last two hours of the flood tide for them to feed, and therefore their travelling time is at a minimum. An angler can expect the fish to be available in what could be termed concentrated numbers in a relatively small area. You may not need to change your station more than once in such a place to maximise your chances. On the other hand, most bars have at least a small portion that is submerged at all times, and whilst individual bass will still congregate on the last of the ebb on the sea side of the bar, as soon as they feel the first change of tide from ebb slack to first flood, they will cross the bar and use the push of the new flood to maximise their travelling time and distance for the smallest amount of energy expended. A bass travelling in such a manner will only spend time investigating major food-holding areas for short periods, and may not think it worthwhile following a weak scent trail. This is a good reason for using fresh bait on a regular basis. What's more, if a fish comes across food at such a time and misses your hook – even though it gave a good bite – it won't come back. It hasn't the time, nor is it worth wasting the energy needed to swim back up tide. Bass stay in the main channel and tidal current as it forces its way up river, and they may travel several miles upstream only stopping to feed in a determined manner when the flood eases off during the last hour. Some very large fish may go as far as the junction of saltwater and the freshwater river proper, but as before, as soon as the main ebb is underway their retreat back to sea is instantaneous. They may spend a little more time checking all the nooks, crannies, and back eddies than they did on their inward passage (and even nose around the entrances to small side creeks on the off chance of a meal), but by the last two hours of the ebb all the fish will be over the bar and out to pastures new. The next tide brings a fresh run of fish back into the estuary. To get the most from estuary fishing, you have to anticipate the route they are likely to take, and place a good choice of bait in their path.

The size of tide is also important, as is observation and timing. On a large tide, fish may choose to run over the bar perhaps one hour after low water. You may have three bites before they are past and you have to move on to maintain contact. On the smaller neaps, when there is a greater volume of water over the bar, fish may make a move as soon as the flood is first felt, feeding occasionally as they go, and within half an hour be turning over a reef 400 or 500 m (400 or 500 yd) downtide. Some will continue up river some may stop and circulate around a harbour, others will nose their way with the flooding tide up side creeks that give access to lugworm and shellfish beds. Some wily big fish will lurk in the shadows of bridge pilings and rocks, lunging out at passing prey. School fish may drop right down with the tide but stay inside the confines of the estuary either in a side eddy at the mouth or in a deeper pocket in the main channel proper. They never advance as far upstream as the adults, though they are more adventurous in exploring side creeks and mudflats, exploiting a food source untapped by the bigger fish.

Schoolies begin to advance up the estuary again with the flooding tide. But there is more to be said about this. Over a long period of time I realised that when I caught adult fish at a bar mark, anglers a quarter or half a mile further upstream caught schoolies at about the same time and then, after a period, began to catch sizeable bass which were obviously the fish that had been in front of me. If I stayed where I was I rarely caught a schoolie. At other times I caught small juveniles while anglers further up caught nothing. A little later the upstream anglers began to catch schoolies and a batch of quality fish showed in front of me. This suggests that small school fish move up the estuary in advance of the adults. On an ebb tide the contrary happens. On the first of the ebb you may catch schoolies for, say, one hour. These then move over the sand banks that line the outer estuary and feed on the beaches facing the outflowing current. After a pause, the adult fish arrive. Should the adults show first you can expect a short burst of activity followed by a lull; then the small bass arrive, to feed in the main channel until dead low water. Always pay attention to a period of inactivity after you've been hitting schoolies – it's a good sign that big fish are present.

The best tides for bass fishing are the biggest springs of all, because then shore crabs are at their most numerous. The crabs feed in the greatest numbers at slack water on a high spring tide during darkness and bass take advantage of this. But the fish are spread over a wide area at such times and it is usually the smaller fish that are caught. I prefer tides of 8–9 m (27–29 ft) on the Liverpool Scale, for these favour the bigger fish (see page 86).

The obvious place and time to begin fishing is on the bar in the last hour of the ebb, when the bass are assembling ready for the first flush of flooding tide that signals the start of their feeding run. Most of them will work the bottom ridge, where the steep angle of the sand bar terminates and the sea bed flattens out. They can be tempted by sand-eels presented on a long, light trace, and held to the bottom by a small weight easily moved around by the agitation of surf and current. It's wise to encourage the weight to work along the bottom of the ridge. Do this by releasing line with the reel in free spool; when a few metres of line have passed through the rod rings place your thumb or finger on the spool. The line will gradually tighten and as it does so the pressure of the tide on the line and weight makes the weight and the eel climb up the incline of the sand bar. Using this technique there is no need to cast more than a few metres, yet you can effectively work a bait huge distances. Even a frozen eel behaves in a natural way – holding station

Small bass taken spinning with a redgill eel from the shore

for short periods then fluttering backwards as the current takes it to new ground. A live sand-eel can be absolutely deadly.

Use a nickel-finished Aberdeen-style hook with a long shank in size 1/0 or 2/0 up to 6/0 (depending on the size of the eel to be used). Insert the point through the eel's lower jaw and push the eel around the bend and a little way up the shank. Lightly nick the point and barb through the eel a little way back from the gill cover – not through the middle of the body but just inside the lower belly line. Alternatively, take the hook through the upper jaw and pass through the whole shank and eye. Nick the eel in the back so that the hook is held lengthways along the back by the line leading through the upper jaw. These methods apply when only a little casting distance is needed. When a greater range is required, I use a small swivel situated at the wrist of the tail, which is secured by a short length of shearing elastic. A 50–75 mm (2–3 in) length of trace line (depending on the size of eel) is added to the lower swivel eye, and the long shanked hook is tied to this. The hook is then inserted mid-body, just behind the gill covers. Ensure that the line between the hook and swivel is slack – if not it may rip out on casting.

A good way of mounting a live sand-eel – and to keep it alive – is simply to pass the hook point through the lower jaw and leave it at that. I try to use the smallest hook I feel sensible at the time, usually a 1/0 or a 2/0. As the hook size increases, so does the weight factor, which in turn impairs the eel's natural manoeuvrability.

Bites are simple, almost savage, affairs. The bass engulfs the eel in one go and then turns sideways into the current, making the line come taut very sharply. Now and then a fish may take the eel and swim forward a metre or so before turning. If you're keeping contact with your lead through the line you feel a momentary loss of tension before the line again draws tight. If you experience this, wait until you feel the fish through the line and just tighten into it.

Sand-eel is a daylight and dusk bait; for fishing over the bar at night or on an early morning tide we must appeal to the fish's sense of smell. You can fish chunks of peeler crab in much the same way as you did the sand-eel, but I prefer to position myself where I can cast to the edge of the main out-flow of water from the estuary, and let the current carry the scent of the crab bait to the waiting fish. You'll need heavier gear, say a light beachcaster and 85–110 g (3–4 oz) lead. Let it run with the current but on a tight line, so that the bait is brought closer to the edge of fast water – this is where the bass are most prone to take. If your lead finds a hollow, leave it there – it has discovered a natural food-holding area undoubtedly frequented by fish. Look out, too, for back eddies, which have undercurrents that encourage food morsels to collect (see Fig. 16).

In rough weather with a good surf running over the bar, fish may well be feeding in the tumbling water before attempting the estuary. No fish will look a gift horse in the mouth if it comes across a piece of peeler, fresh razor, or even a couple of lug on a 4/0. Use a short hook link to give the bait some stability. In easy or moderate surf, use a wandering lead to seek the fish out. In a good blow and heavy surf, fish static with a wired lead.

It's important to move before the turn of the tide to a pre-chosen mark inside the estuary where you feel bass will pass. If the bar is covered by constant water, your bait must be lying in wait for the fish to find as they pass through. Coming over the bar they'll choose the deepest part of the channel but they'll quickly move out to work the edges where the current may have deposited food. This is where you must place your bait. A better bet still is to find a patch of seed mussel or of broken ground and place your bait just above, so that the tide takes the scent from your bait across the very ground the fish is working. It still pays to 'match the hatch', so peeler or soft crab is a natural choice. If the water is fairly shallow but water currents have created deeper holes, try to drop the bait into one of these or at the base of a miniature drop-off.

As the tide increases and the water spreads over the whole width of the estuary, fish become more scattered. Many will work the flanks, picking over broken ground and swimming along sand-bank edges to see what they

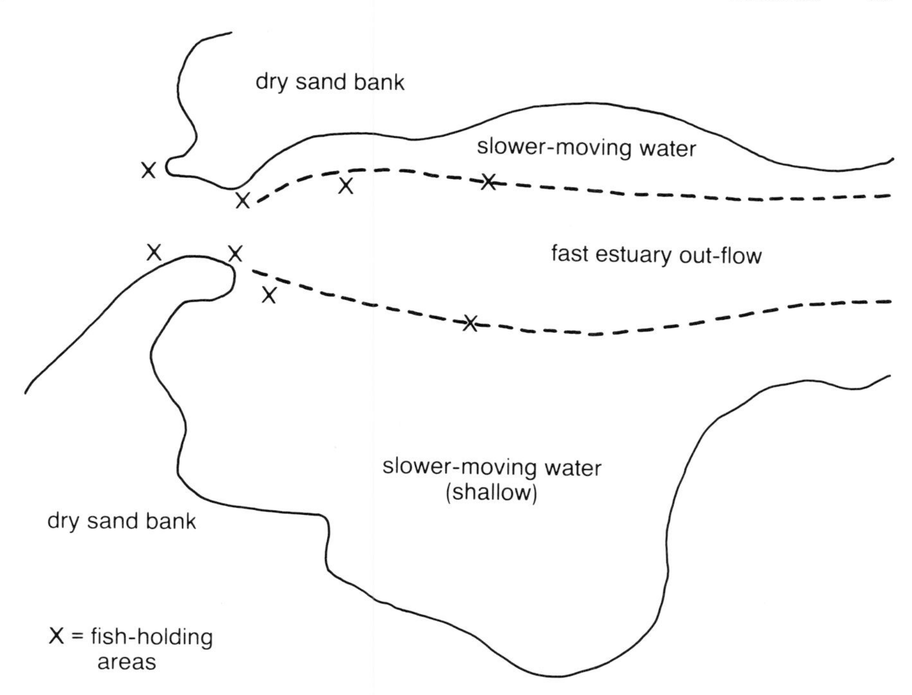

Fig. 16
Estuary bar and out-flow fish postions

can disturb in the way of small fish and shrimps. Don't neglect the main channel, where the strongest current still runs, as the bigger fish are likely to be here. You may have to employ long-range casting, with distances in excess of 90 m (100 yd) to stay in contact with this natural motorway, but it's a good place to rest a bait. None the less, keep an eye open for back eddies and broken patches or places where the leading edge of a sand-bank causes friction in the water. An area of choppy or white water at the edge of a current will always attract fish.

When the flooding tide in the main channel is restricted by a narrow gap there will be deeper water and beds of mussel and rock will be deposited on each flank. On the smaller neaps the neck of this natural funnel will fish well, but on the spring tide, when the flow of water may reach 4 or 5 knots, the current will be too strong for fish to swim against and they let themselves be borne along with it and begin to search for food again only when the flow eases. In such a situation the angler must locate the area where the food that is washed through this funnel is deposited downtide. It is usually at a bend in the main channel or on the edge of a major sand bank, where an undercurrent holds and creates a larder. The top of a submerged sand bank just off the main current will hold sand-eels and small fish that are washed through the tide run, and it pays to let your bait run up the leading edge of this bank and settle on top. Remember that the top of the bank will show choppy white water, but this will be a few metres down from the bank, so aim to drop your bait slightly uptide for a perfect position. Such a place presents the opportunity to free-line a live sand-eel

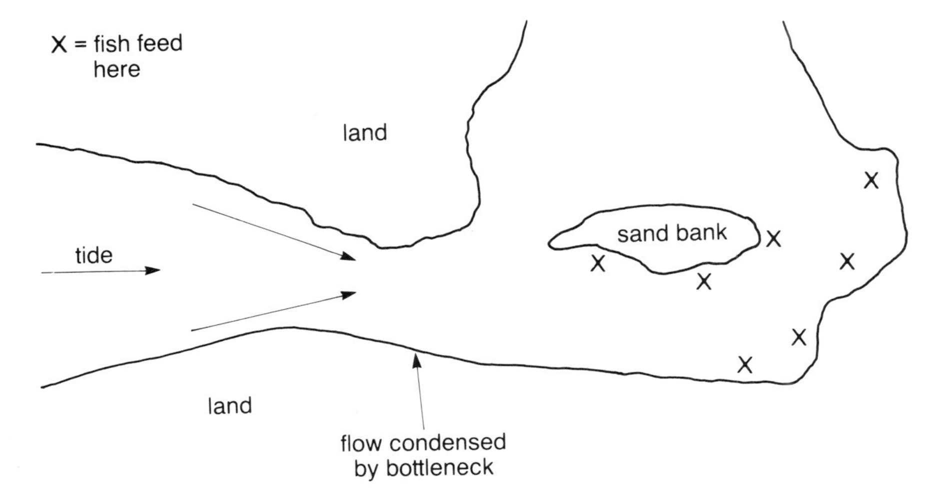

Fig. 17
Estuary bottleneck

down-current and over the bank (see Fig. 17). Any obstacle, natural or man-made, will draw fish. Estuaries often have small harbours where local fishing boats deposit the waste from their commercial catches and bass will be drawn by the small baitfish and crabs that feast on this freebie. The harbour walls have numerous cracks in the stonework where crabs take up residence. Expect bass to nose around these. Piers and jetties are good places for bass, especially if there is tide run through and around the piles. The flow of tide digs holes and gutters around these supports, where the bass can find crabs and sand-eels. Use a long, flowing trace and cast just above the piles so that the bait wafts temptingly around the hollows at their base. Deep troughs, enclosed by high banks of sand, tend to connect the bridge or jetty supports. Fish will have to use up very little energy to hold station in these troughs while the tide brings their food to them.

By all means take advantage of any lie that enables you to free-line a live bait down to this area, though in a quick and rapid current you may need some lead to gain enough depth. During the main holiday weeks, when numerous inexperienced fathers and sons line the jetty, many small fish and crabs become casualties of inexpert handling. At dusk some bass may move in to clean up the bodies, so a static deadbait or fish chunk can be utilised.

In daytime, and if the water is fairly clear, bass rarely run the estuary at all. Some may, but they will change their habits. They will take advantage of every scrap of cover, hanging around weed beds and waiting under the hulls of craft moored in the shallows, pouncing on anything edible that strays within range.

Areas of sandflats or spartina marshes are drained by numerous side creeks and run-offs. As the tide fills the main channel and spills out to drown first the creeks and small inlets, and ultimately the sandflats themselves, so some bass edge their way up these drainage gullies searching for crabs and worms. Usually the last two hours of the flood are most productive. I've always found the very mouths of such places to be

The depressions caused by tidal effect and scouring action around bridge and pier supports – ideal ground for bass

excellent. Tidal flows can often be strong and you may have to use a fair-sized lead. The best presentation is on a flowing trace 1.25 m (4 ft) or more long. The bass will come when the creek entrance has enough water for them to cross unobserved. You can fish higher up the creeks with success using tactics similar to those for the main channels, keeping baits close into the steep sides. It's safe to say that the fish will travel as far as you can find crabs up the tideline.

As the tide peaks, fish will be turning over the rock and weed areas at the high-tide marks along the full length of the estuary. The ground where you found your crab baits at low water is where the bass are at high water. At night baits placed only 3 m (10 ft) from shore in such places may find a victim. If you haven't too much water movement, a free-lined piece of peeler swung out into 60 cm (2 ft) of water can be deadly – it's exactly what the fish expects to find.

As the tide retreats, so do the bass. They drop back along the drainage gullies into the major channels, sometimes stopping to investigate the odd nook and cranny. Most bass cross the bar back to the open sea during the middle two hours of the ebb, few fish stay longer, whatever the size of the tide. Estuaries with deeper water that always covers the bar may hold fish in their mouths until the last of the ebb if there is some natural food-holding area such as a reef or mussel bed. During times of heavy rainfall, when the estuary water is brown and full of impurities from the land, bass will stay near the mouth. Here the salinity suits them and they can intercept food forms borne down from the estuary. When the rains cease only after two or perhaps three tides will there be good fishing again. Then, as the water clears a take often comes within thirty seconds of the bait settling on the seabed.

In more northerly climes it's rare to find many adult bass in the estuaries before late May and it is usually not until June that they arrive in great numbers. These estuaries, fed by mountain streams and rivers, carry melting snow waters until mid-April and only then begin to warm up. In the south things may move a little earlier. The juveniles appear around the third week of April and remain until the end of the year. The bigger fish arrive from early to mid-May. July and August see the bass far offshore working the baitfish shoals, though there's the odd good fish still using the estuaries with the youngsters. Late August sees good numbers of fish back in the estuaries feeding up for the coming winter and it's at this time that the largest fish are taken. By the end of September or early October the adults are away on their southerly migration. An Indian summer can hold them for a week longer, but this is clutching at straws. On the south coast the season is extended until mid-November, and the odd fish (usually large) may show at any time throughout the winter.

A few extra hints to close this chapter. In times of rough weather and gales dense blankets of weed ascend the estuaries, but you can still enjoy some sport by fishing at high-and-low-water slack. Estuaries can fish very well at times of hard onshore blows, when even the larger, more powerful fish find the quieter estuary waters more to their liking. If you see salmon and seatrout tailing and leaping, you'll have no hope of taking bass, except a few small ones. Adult bass and game fish won't run the estuary together, perhaps because they like different barometric pressures and water conditions.

Never display yourself more than you have to, even in the dark. An angler is starkly silhouetted against a pale moonlit overcast sky. Don't wade at night until you have fished the near water, otherwise you may scare fish feeding or swimming close in. When wading at low water on a bar or sand bank perhaps several hundred metres away from the high-tide mark, be ever observant that the tide doesn't cut you off. To get the most from estuary bassing you must master the art of ambush and interception, waylaying the bass as it makes its way upriver. Don't carry excess tackle, stay manoeuvrable, and follow the fish.

6 Boat Fishing

During the summer months, at times of high barometric pressure and offshore winds, bass move offshore, shoaling up in huge numbers to attack baitfish shoals. This happens where there are areas of rough, shallow ground, where jagged reef systems poke their heads to within a metre or so of the surface, where tide races are present off headlands, and around estuary mouths. The baitfish shoals always swim into the oncoming wind.

Bass have other favourite food-gathering areas – shallow sand banks far out to sea that create an increase in tidal flow; any areas of rocky, rubbly ground within a half mile of the shore; and weedbeds with the occasional sand patch. Long finger-like reef systems running outwards from beaches may point the route taken by bass as the tide turns and the first of the flood gets underway. Wrecks that lie close inshore will yield big bass; so, from time to time, will deep-water wrecks. Sewer out-falls lying 360 or 450 m (400 or 500 yd) offshore are again excellent hunting grounds. Always, the prerequisite of good bassing is to find good food-holding features that draw the fish within range of your bait.

Bass are lovers of fast, lively water so when boat fishing attention to safety is important. Always wear a good life-jacket. Carry plenty of flares and renew them at regular intervals. Always have a spare motor capable of getting you home from your furthest mark. Carry a few likely spares such as spark plugs and shear pins and some basic tools. Extra fuel is a must, but store it only in tightly-sealed metal containers, never plastic ones. Take three oars not two – oars may be lost and you can't get much propulsion with one oar. Carry two plastic buckets to act as bailers in case you take on water. Have an anchor rope four times as long as the greatest depth expected and use good quality chain to link it to the anchor. At least two anchors are needed, one for sand and one for rough bottoms. If finances allow, the installation of a radio to give some shore contact is more important than a sounder to locate marks. When fishing, keep the interior of the craft clean to avoid slipping – a large bin or plastic bowl keeps fish slime at bay and is easy to wash out. All used items of equipment should be returned to their lodgings immediately they are no longer needed – loose equipment causes falls, leading to broken limbs and bashed heads and a possible person overboard. Have some means of audible warning in case of poor visibility; the aerosol horns beloved of yacht-racing starting officials are reasonably priced and eminently suitable. Always tell a reliable person – a coastguard, harbourmaster, or a member of your family – what craft you are taking, how many people are aboard, what areas you intend to fish, and your expected time of arrival back at the quay or slipway.

Don't make a small craft unstable by standing up in it any more than you have to – if possible, remain seated even when retrieving the anchor. When dropping the anchor, don't throw out the hook and chain in one parcel – the chain often becomes knotted around the anchor, causing all sorts of obvious problems. Get the anchor over the side and gently pay out the chain through your hands; when you come to the rope you can let gravity do the rest. Mark the anchor rope at 7.5-m (25-ft) intervals with differently coloured strings or with paint, then if you know the depth of water you know how much rope to release. When you come to be more proficient at boat handling and you know exactly where to position your craft for ideal placement over a fish holding mark you can use the length of anchor rope to adjust and reposition for optimum effect.

Modern fish-location devices certainly make life easier and are always of value on board but they are capable of surveying only a small piece of sea bed at any one time. It's up to you, as the skipper, to pick the most likely general area as a bass-holding spot, then use the sounder to locate a hot-spot within a hot-spot.

On shore you can observe much of the ground you will be fishing because the tide uncovers it at low water, but to gather information for marks at sea you have to use other methods. Good boat marks are as jealously guarded as good shore marks so questions – such as where, when, how far, and what with? – are unlikely to receive a polite and truthful answer. More devious methods must be employed.

If you're inland based, then read the catch reports in fishing papers and magazines and try to identify through them areas that hold some promise. The choice is easier if, like me, you are fortunate enough to live on the coast. Then a few evenings on the local quay will prove valuable. Watch the boats coming in. If you see one showing off a good day's catch, make sure you can recognise it again. Don't comment or appear overly-interested, but keep your eyes and ears open. If one boat seems consistently to do better than most, try to anticipate its next trip, find a vantage point, and, using binoculars, try to watch where it anchors. At least this helps you identify general areas. If this direct approach isn't possible, note the boat's outward bearing and general course. Slowly you can build up a picture of the areas favoured by the more successful boats. Once out there you can anchor in different parts of the area and select the best hot-spots. Under no circumstances should you fish in close proximity to a craft already anchored – that angler has beaten you to it and you should go elsewhere.

Once you have pinpointed a good fishing spot, find it again by using land features such as buildings or trees as line-up markers. I always use three easily distinguishable features, one off the bow and two that line up off the port and starboard sides. One bow and one side marker will do if you're good at judging distances.

If you're going solo, the first step is to purchase the admiralty chart that gives your chosen piece of coast in the greatest detail. You can use the chart to eliminate all the areas of flat-pan sand and to find rocky areas, gravel patches that denote some tide run, and sand banks that show a sharp rise from an otherwise boring seabed. Look for a long, low shelf leading towards the beach – bass will follow it along its lower edge. A rocky headland that juts out into the sea across the direct path of the tide creates a brisk tide race; the bass will use its fast currents to pick off small fish that have been sucked into it and swept away by the force of water. Rock pinnacles that reach for the surface may hold the odd good bass partial to a sand-eel. Major and minor reef systems reaching out to the depths are good for shoaling bass in summer. Any area that suggests the tide flow may be tunnelled or forced through a bottleneck should be earmarked for evaluation – take your binoculars and from high ground on a rough day look for water that shows more motion than the surrounding area and on calm sunny days, when the sea is clear and the sky holds few clouds to cast shadows, look for the darker patches in the shallower water that give away weed and rough-ground positions. When afloat on a flat, oily calm day you will see the surface of the water change as you cross the line of sand on to rough ground. The surface water above the rough becomes more ripply and often has a close and minute chop – the rougher the weather the more this line of change becomes visible.

Near estuary mouths bass will travel the very edge of coloured estuarine water as it flows out of the mouth, while staying in the more neutral non-tainted water. Still close inshore, but in deep water, a small wreck on an otherwise dull bed will have its head of bass, even the weed growth that adorns man-made undersea out-falls or pipelines could prove a worthwhile proposition. Bass often appear around freshly laid and baited lobster pots, and anywhere that commercial fishing craft dump unwanted fish and offal. To fish these locations, many shore-fishing techniques can be adapted for use from the boat with a little modification and thought.

Many parts of the rough-ground bass beaches described on pages 31–34 are inaccessible to a person on foot and never see a hook. Approached from the seaward side they can yield rich rewards. The water will be shallow, and you need to keep a careful look out for rocks. Be as quiet as you can – cut the engine a good distance away from the spot to be fished, using the oars to complete the final stage. Once in position, take extra care not to drop leads on the deck or make heavy footfalls. It's a good idea to be in position before you think the fish will show – in other words, to wait in ambush. The ideal position is with the boat a simple 27 or 37-m (30 or 40-yd) lob from some broken ground or the base of a boulder.

A long rod such as a carp or spinning rod is perfect – it is capable of casting up to 85 g (3 oz) at a push, while its length gives better control than the more conventional, stiff boat rods as well as better bite indication.

I don't change my end gear much from the shore rig for the same situation. A 60-cm (2-ft) drop to the lead with a short link is excellent – though, if you're fussy, you can shorten the lead link to 30 cm (1 ft) and lengthen the hook trace to around 60 cm (2 ft). This won't tangle unduly yet offers free acceptance to a fish while retaining good bite detection (see Fig. 18).

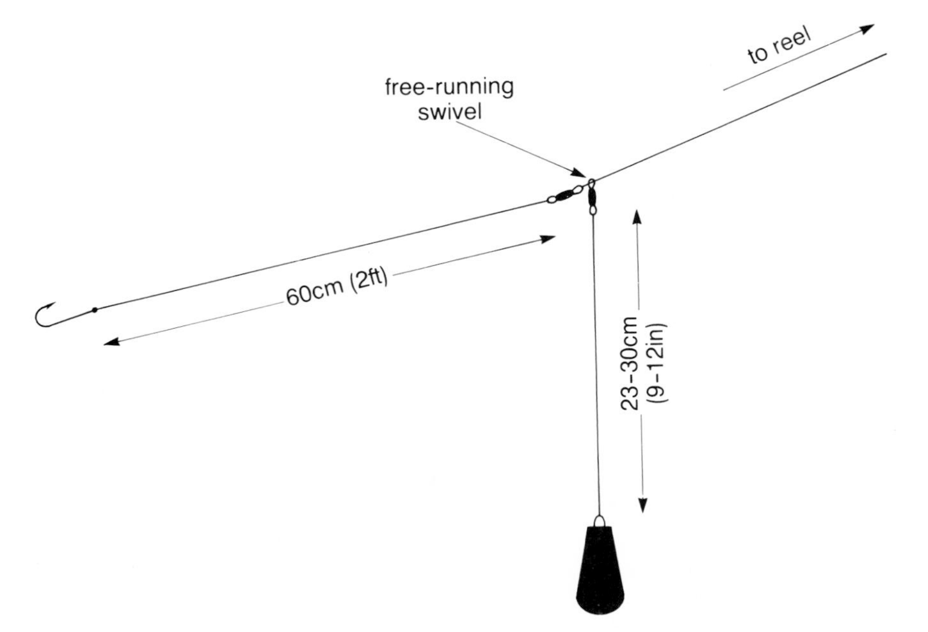

Fig. 18
Shallow ground bait-trace

In rough, coloured water I use a fixed trace but in calm, clear seas I use the free-running version. Bait is once more the peeler crab. Squid is useful for outsize fish. It is possible to trot a bait downtide on float gear, and this is worth a try as a change of technique, but in my experience it gives no better results. There will only be two or three bites at any mark before the fish move on; a move a few hundred metres downtide may relocate them.

Inshore and offshore sand banks are bound to be home to numerous sand-eels and the bass won't be far behind. They will be on the downtide side of the sand bank in the quieter water, where the passing current will bring them lunch. The positioning of the boat is not as straightforward a matter as some may think. The general concensus is that the craft should be positioned directly above the bank, so that the bait can be free-lined or trotted down to the fish. Providing the push of tide is not too fast, fishing in this way can be effective. If the tide run is fast, though, it may be dangerous to try to anchor in this position and any fish hooked have to be dragged back against the flow of tide, reducing a pleasurable fight with (one hopes) a powerful fish into an unpleasant winching session. It makes far more sense to place the boat slightly uptide and slightly to one side of the sand bank so that the bait can be cast with a light lead on to the top of the sand bank's leading edge. The tide will then sweep it down the bank. Most bites will come as the bait is being brought round by the pressure of the tide on the line. If the bank's gradient is gentle it pays to cast the bait, still with a lightish lead, on to the top of the bank. Have the reel in free spool and every 10 seconds or so release 0.9–1.2 m (3–4 ft) of line. Again, the lead will describe a huge arc. The bites will come when the just-released line begins to tighten and it's then a simple matter to re-engage the spool and tighten into the fish (see Fig. 19).

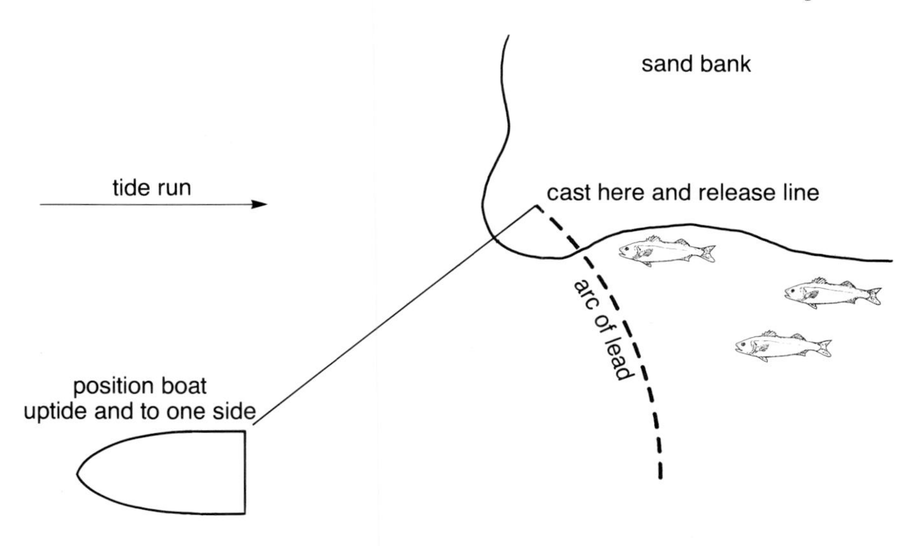

Fig. 19
Boat position

By sitting the boat outside the main flow of water but casting into it you increase your chances of landing fish, for once a fish is hooked it will use the passing water current to good effect, but with the rod at an angle to this flow (rather than uptide and in line with it) it will be drawn away from this flow into quieter water behind the boat, where the fight will be a little less one-sided.

The sand-eel is the best bait, but king rag used in lengths of 15–20 cm (6–8 in) with 5 or 8 cm (2 or 3 in) left to flutter is also very good. The lead needs to be heavy enough to stay put against the current but light enough to be bounced slowly downtide. Use the longest trace you can handle. By alternately releasing and holding the line, you will give your bait the appearance of a live eel behaving naturally – quietly holding station one minute, then letting the tide drift it back a metre or so the next.

If you find a sand bank parallel with the tidal flow you can anchor the boat a short way uptide and cast your bait on to the facing edge of the bank, say two-thirds of the way up. It's here that the bass tend to feed. You can still use the rolling-ledger method, but it is equally effective to use uptide gear and wired-release leads to hold your bait firm. Bites usually register as a couple of taps, then the lead pulls clear from its grip in the sand. Hooked fish often run towards you, so if all goes slack, reel in quickly to regain contact – your obvious reaction that the fish is lost is most often the wrong one. Rough ground in deepish water can be sometimes good and sometimes bad. The boat should be anchored with its stern 55–70 m (60–80 yd) beyond your chosen mark so that the bait can be trotted down to the fish. A large chunk of edible peeler crab bounced downtide on a 2.1–2.4-m (7–8-ft) trace will be eagerly accepted (see Fig. 20).

Other good baits are a large mackerel fillet, a markerel head with the backbone and one fillet attached, and a whole pouting. Use a long trace but keep the free-running swivel that holds the lead in your hand while you release the bait into the tide along with 6–9 m (20–30 ft) of line. Clove-

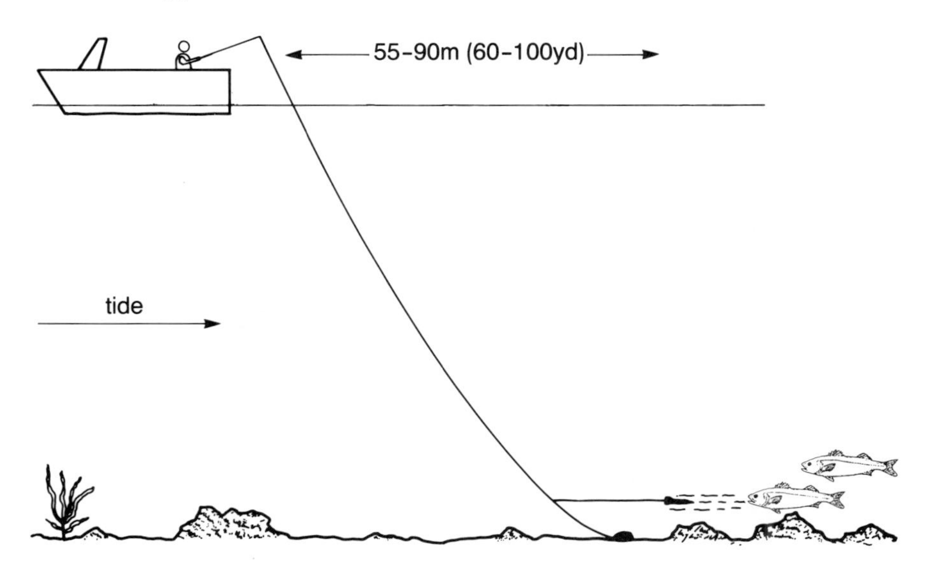

Fig. 20
Boat position

hitch a matchstick into the line or tie on an elastic band to act as a stop. Tie a piece of mono about 2.5–3 m (8–10 ft) long to the eye of the free-running swivel and the lead to the opposite end. Lower the lead over the side and, as you trot it away from the stern of the boat, it will stay near the bottom, but the bait will flutter 0.9–1.2 m (3–4 ft) over the top of the rough/ground, proving irresistible to the feeding bass. When the matchstick reaches the rod ring it will snap (if it hasn't already done so during the fight); the rubber band will just fold double and run through the rings onto the reel. The free-running swivel slides down until it hits the trace swivel.

To mount the deadbait I insert the hook through the mouth and down through the gullet, bringing it out through the side of the fillet. With bigger baits I bring the hook point through the gill cover, giving a strong mounting point and excellent hooking on the strike. I always wire the jaws together to stop water coming into the mouth and spinning the bait. Takes feel as though tidal pressure has suddenly eased, then, equally suddenly, all comes tight (see Fig. 21).

You can use the same technique with squid as bait, but I prefer then to use a Pennel tackle (two hooks mounted on the same trace). Apart from increasing hooking power, two hooks prevent the squid ending up in an unsightly blob around the gape of a hook. Use the squid whole; with its legs free to move in the current it will look natural and carry some scent.

Any small ridges near estuary mouths or just below the low-water line off some beaches are worth trying, especially at low water. Again, it's simply a matter of working the bait down to the ridge edge and letting it drop where it will be swept around by the current. Long traces will, as before, give the most natural presentation.

Sewer pipes or out-falls carrying drainage water away from beaches always hold the bass's interest and it's a simple matter to position the boat just uptide of the pipe's mouth. The passing tide running over and across the pipe creates a miniature tide race, which will hold fish when no effluent is being discharged. As soon as pumping starts the fish will move out into the clearer water but feed on the edge of the outgoing spill. Around the pipe's outlet a hole or hollow will have formed that will hold small flatfish; these, in turn, will draw the bigger bass. If the pipe is part of a construction braced by boulders or concrete there should be a few crabs around. Try following the pipe beachwards and casting a bait or ledgering a piece of peeler at the base of any part of the construction that is facing into the tide.

Wrecks, providing they're not too far from shore, will hold a consistent head of bass. It's not only the abundant baitfish present around the superstructure that draws them to feed, there will also be a supply of peelers – mainly edible crabs but, depending on the depth and distance from shore, the occasional shore crab as well.

Position your boat directly uptide, so that when the anchor rope pulls tight the stern is 70–100 m (75–100 yd) from the sunken hull. Tidal flow and speed must, though, be taken into consideration – on slack neaps anchor right over the top of the wreck.

Baits, which should be edible peelers or sizeable chunks of mackerel, should be trotted down to rest alongside the vessel – though baits fished on the bottom are likely to draw a succession of nuisance fish. The deadbait technique described for rough ground (see page 67) is ideal for presenting a fish with a fairly natural meal. It's also a good method of displaying a livebait, if your conscience doesn't trouble you. Tackle loss may be high, but so is the average size of fish caught. I don't like to fish when there's more than, say, 25 m (80 ft) of water over these hulls and I favour marks within about a mile of the beach.

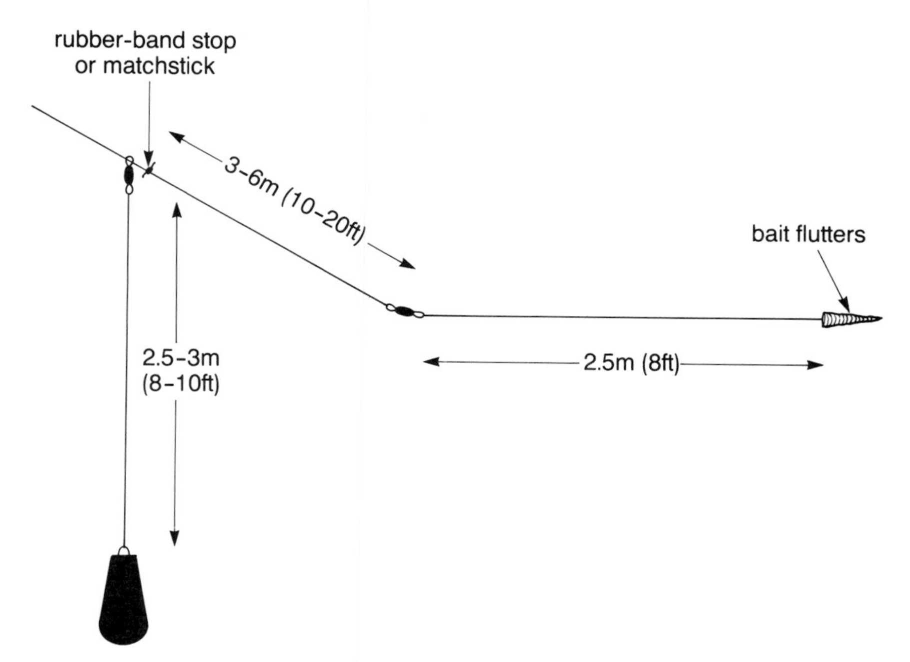

Fig. 21
Long boat-trace

Fishing over dense kelp beds is productive, as bass delight in nosing through the stalks with their eyes ever-vigilant for some tasty fish or crustacean. Some anglers who fish weedbed marks complain of tackle loss and small catches, but that is because they stick to the standard boat tackle of running paternoster with a long trace. Obviously they are not going to find many bass – their baits are hidden in a jungle of weed. Use a metal or plastic boom and experiment with the distance you set it from the lead – the ideal setting is when the bites become most frequent! A long trace will make the bait flutter enticingly over and around the tops of the weed stalks. Attach the lead with a short length of very weak line, then if it should become fast you only lose the weight. When you hook into a fish in this type of terrain it pays to hustle it a metre or so off the bottom and control the fight in mid-water (see Fig. 22).

Fast, aerated water always draws bass and jagged offshore pinnacle reefs are favourite haunts. Huge shoals of launce inhabit such areas and bass shoal up to make the most of this opportunity. Only two techniques pay dividends – floatfishing or free-lining live sand-eels or trolling redgills through the turbulent water.

Remember that these reefs are the graveyards of many ships; rocks concealed a metre or so under the surface can rip a hole in the hull. It is best to go out first with a charter skipper. After a season or so of regular trips,

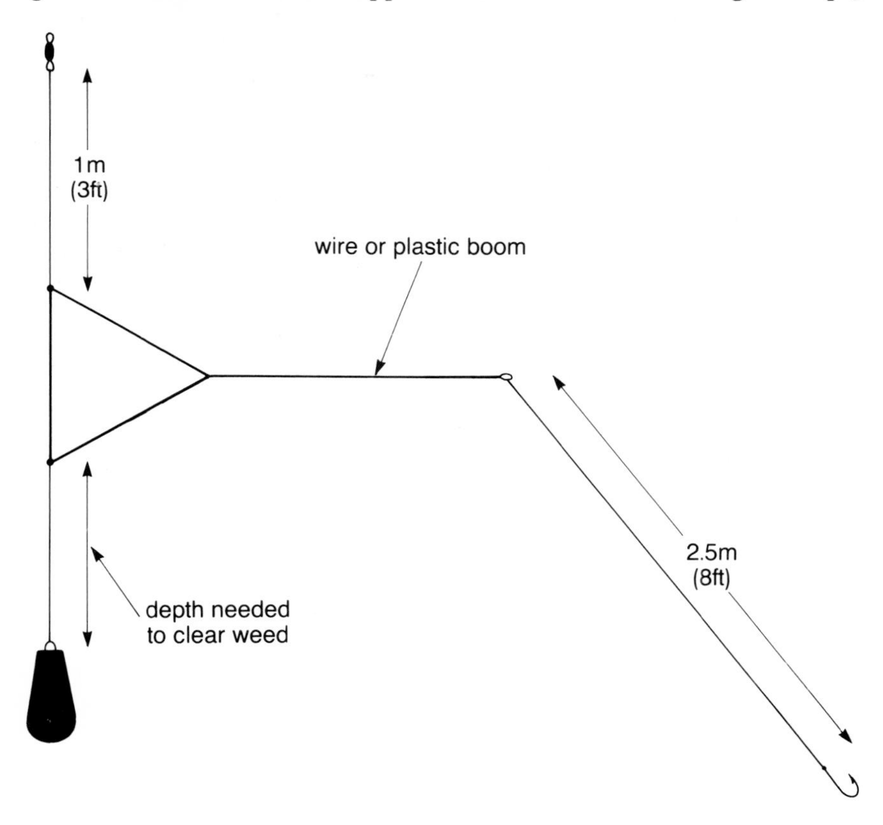

Fig. 22
Wire boom-rig for weedbeds

you can have a go in your own craft. Drifting with an idling motor is fairly standard practice and presents a free-lined eel to perfection. The shoals of launce are forced to the surface by the bass or other feeding fish; you can see that the feeding frenzy is in progress from the slashing and boiling of the launce as they turn and dive. I leave my reel in free spool and gently let line trickle out. At the first sign of a take I leave my left thumb clamped around the spool to stop it revolving and, as I lift the rod, crank the reel into gear with my right hand. There is no need to strike; just let the rod assume its fighting curve as the fish turns away. Make sure the clutch is lightly set because the heavy water gives an already powerful fish an added turn of speed. Avoid standard boat rods – it's much better to use a carp or spinning rod or an uptider.

A similar system can be worked with the float, but you then have the extra comfort of being able to fish the eel at a pre-set depth. This is useful, because the biggest fish will often be at the base of the shoal. Use a biggish cylindrical float, select your drop, and fix your stop above the float. (A rubber band is all you need.) Have a loose round bullet big enough to cock the float running free on the line and stop this with a large swivel. To the swivel tie a 1.2 or 1.5-m (4 or 5-ft) long trace and add your eel. Bites are very decisive – the float just disappears. Again, have the reel in attended free spool and engage as the fish comes up tight.

Black is a good colour to paint a float. Bright yellow and orange are sometimes hard to see against a choppy sea. Stick to cylindrical polystyrene floats because these offer less resistance to a taking fish than old pike bungs. Also, because they are long, by careful choice of lead weight you can set them high and make them still more visible. A redgill rubber eel worked free-line or with some added weight is excellent trundled down with the current then brought back with the occassional upsweep of the rod.

Trolling redgills is ideal in the less-fierce tidal runs of inshore reefs, when the bass head for these during the summer lull of July and August. Tackle set-up is easy and any other method used produces a drop in results. Bass and their food source on such occasions are always just below the surface. Tie a largish swivel direct to your main line and add a trace of 16 kg (35 lb) mono say 1.8 m (6 ft) long and add the redgill. Free-line this at least 70 m (75 yd) away from the boat. You feel a relatively gentle tightening as the bass engulfs the eel. There is no need to strike. As you hook up, shout for the engine to be cut and play the fish. The other anglers in the boat should reel in slowly, as other bass are likely to hang themselves on as the eels are being retrieved. White eels are good during lightish conditions but in coloured seas and in low light a black gill is even better. Stick with these two colours and you won't go far wrong. The best size is the 172 mm, which will take everything from schoolies to lunkers.

When trolling, there's no need to keep jigging the rod as you would for mackerel; the steady pull of the boat is enough, ABU Toby spoons in the 28-g (1-oz) size and above are effective, but in fact any lure that wriggles and writhes will at some time prove a winner. Trolling speeds may vary – somewhere between fast tickover and 2½ to 3 knots is about right. Cloudy conditions are best, as bright sunshine sends the fish deep. Don't troll along

A nearly 4-kg (9-lb) bass caught using an artificial eel trolled from a boat in Cardigan bay

the reef's length, it's better to zigzag across it. On quieter days takes may come as the eel is being brought round at the centre of the turning circle. On larger boats, if three or four anglers are fishing the stern, make sure you all fish at different distances and beware of tangles on the turning arc. Trolling over shallow wrecks finds far more bass than anchoring and working the eel on the rod, which is fairly ineffective, but you will need to add some weight to your trace to fish the eel deep enough.

Trolling is successful in estuaries over rough ground and around mussel beds, usually when the tide is at peak run – catches drop off as the tide eases. The mouths and bars of such places are worth covering with the artificial eel as well (see Fig. 23). The methods described (pages 56–57, 58 and 60) for fishing estuaries work for boat fishing, where you can get to marks unreachable from the shore.

Always exhaust the bass, draw them to the quiet water at the stern, and net them. Carry the biggest net you can find – many specimen carp nets are

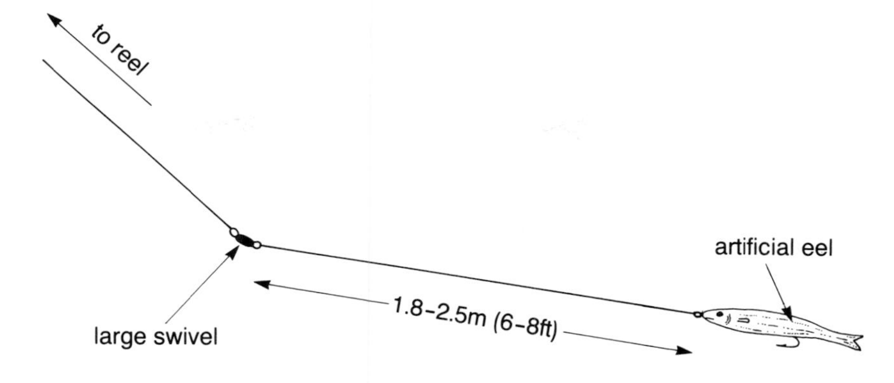

Fig. 23
Trolling rig for boats

ideal. The safest way is to have the net pre-sunk and ease the fish over the net and, in one clean lift, engulf it tail first. If the head of the bass hangs over the rim you're in trouble, but to try to net it head first. It means a broken trace and lost fish if it goes wrong. Never be tempted to drag a fish in by the trace and don't hassle a fish against the current – gentle, persuasive pressure is time-consuming but more effective.

For those of you who use the facilities of a charter boat, it is always beneficial to have and maintain a good relationship with a reliable boat skipper.

7 Spinners and Plugs

Compared to the United States, Britain is still far behind when it comes to the use and design of artificial lures. Recent years have seen a slight increase in the use of artificials in Britain, but it is surprising how many anglers admit to never having caught a fish, let alone a bass, on a man-made bait. Because bass are predatory they are ideal subjects for the lure – even small school fish have the predatory instinct and readily eat small fish and sand-eels. Using a lure allows us to fish when there is no time to collect bait and, providing we choose a sensible time of day to lob a lure, in no way lessens our chances of hooking a fish.

Spinning and plug fishing are techniques for close-quarters angling – at times, like the river-trout angler, you can select a cruising fish and drop the lure on its nose. Plugs in particular are effective when fished close in to rocky shores. The venues we've already fished onshore are all suitable for spinning, but the rocky shore offers the best opportunities.

Some understanding of what fish see and how light penetrates water will help us choose the most appropriate lures for a given mark and time. The bass's eyes are large, to receive as much light as possible, and capable of working independently of each other, giving the fish almost 360° of vision. A bass swimming between rocks or through dense weed fronds is capable not only of seeing what is in front of it but also a fleeing fish that the bass has swum past and missed – maximising opportunities. Most fish have some colour vision – often they will show a marked preference for one particular colour of lure.

Fish see through a window that is coned in shape. The width of this avenue of light is ruled by the depth at which the fish is swimming. Close to the surface the fish's area of view is quite small, and only objects passing directly overhead or in close proximity will be noticed. When the fish is swimming much deeper, the field of vision is extended. A fish lying deep down, viewing the world through its cone-shaped window, would see all the objects that stand above the water radiating outwards in its circle of vision. This visual image relies upon a calm, still water surface, with no wind, if some detail is to be evident. On less calm days, when the surface is rippled or choppy, these images merge and became incoherent, governed in degree by the prevailing weather conditions. From this it's easy to see that an angler may not be seen by a fish cruising the surface only 3 or 4 m (10 or 13 ft) out if the angler crouches low on the edge of the water, but if the angler stands up, then a combination of movement and silhouette will alarm the fish (see Fig. 24). If the water is still and clear an angler approaching the water's edge may well be seen by, and frighten off, a bass swimming several metres down. Light travelling into the depths is quickly diffused; it becomes almost non-existent at about 50 m (160 ft) – see Fig. 25.

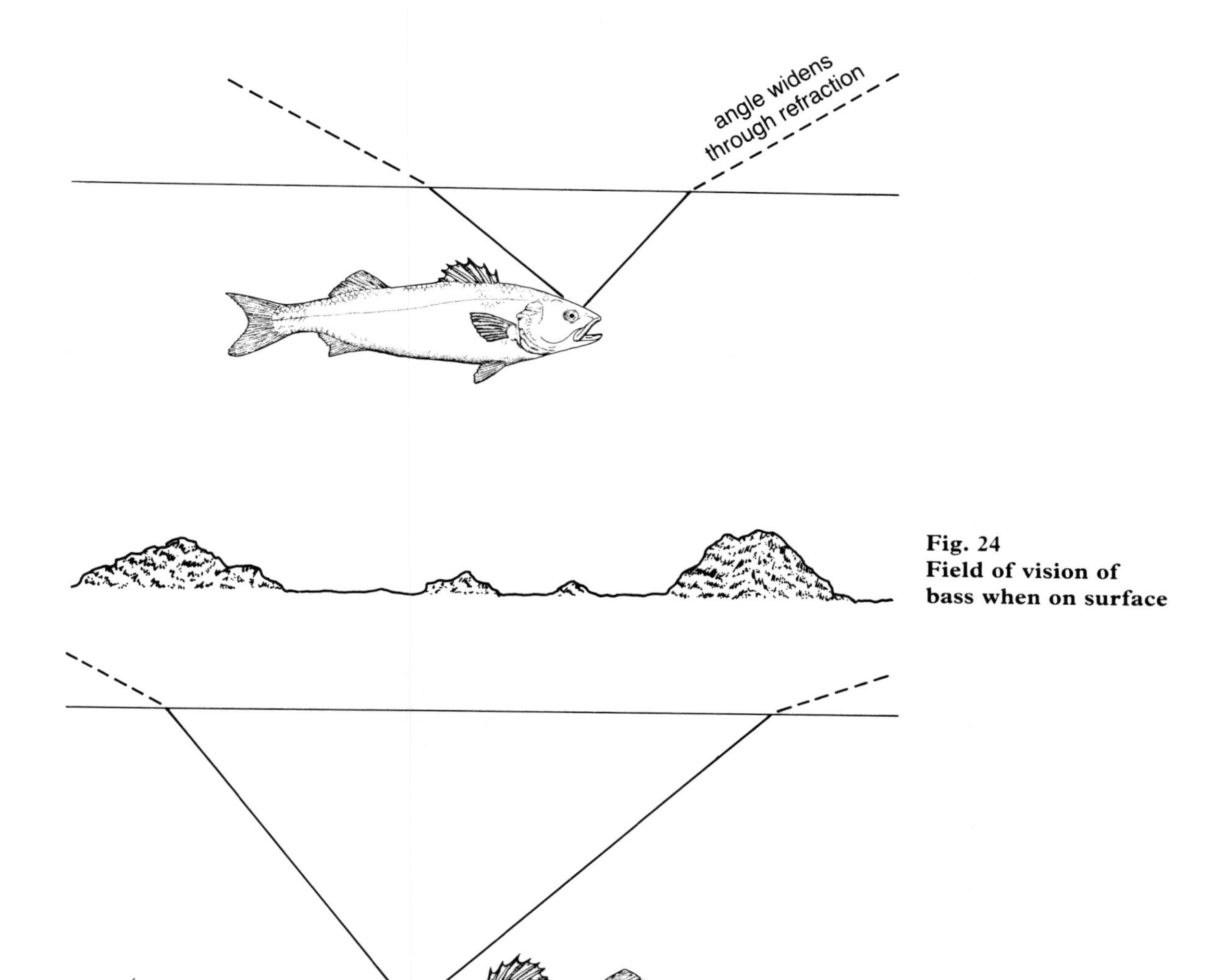

Fig. 24
Field of vision of bass when on surface

Fig. 25
Field of vision widens as bass goes deeper

The time of day (in relation to the angle of the sun) plays a great part in how fish see their meals, and also in the choice of lure colour. Bright sunlight and calm seas at approximately mid-day mean that the sun's rays – being directly overhead – penetrate at their best, giving the fish their greatest detail of vision. This is one reason why to trying to catch fish under these conditions is far from easy. The bass probably see baitfish because the sun's rays reflect on their scales, the bass being drawn by the constant flashes of silver as the little fish dart and turn. It's not surprising, therefore, to find that the best spinners used at such times have silver patches with the majority of the body blacked out. Rubber eels and such like are easily seen by the fish to be fraudulent, and so best left in the box – unless you're fishing deep water where the light levels are low. As the sun drops to the horizon, many anglers will tell you that this is the best time of all to fish – but few know why (see Fig. 26).

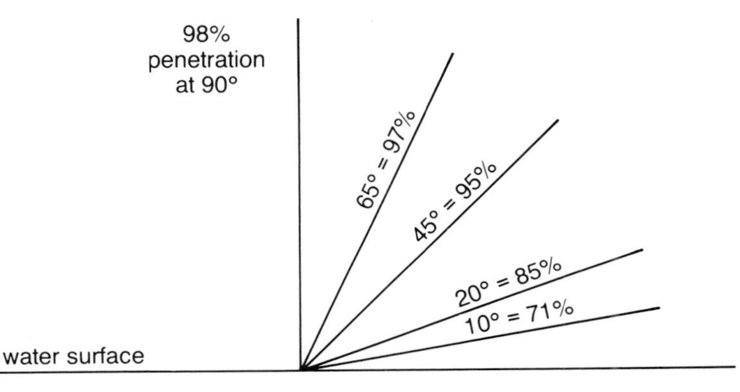

Fig. 26
Light penetration by angles

The shallower the angle of light that hits the water's surface, the more light is reflected or bounced off. Penetration levels fall. Instead of the bass seeing tiny little flashes of silver scales, the best it can hope for is a silhouette or black shadow as a potential food source moves overhead or through the field of vision. The more the light level falls the darker the lures should be. At night black redgills are excellent – they are so, too, even during the day if the surface of the sea is rough and choppy and light levels below are poor. Silver toby spoons and similar may still be effective, as might silver-bodied plugs.

If the water holds some colour and vision is down to a minimum, use a large, white redgill for maximum visibility. I believe that the wagging tail of the redgill eel gives off some vibration, and that the bass picks this up through its lateral line system. Some experiments I've done with night-time spinning and plug fishing show – conclusively, to my mind – that lures that have a wriggle either through the tail of an eel or a double-jointed plug produce fish when light levels are almost nil. Some anglers talk about 'pollack light', which occurs in the evenings over rock marks and the like. During the day catches can be very mediocre, but as the light level falls so the fish feed better. What's happening, I believe, is that during the day the

Two bass taken in the pitch dark after midnight on a redgill eel – their weights were 2.5 kg and 3 kg (5 lb 8 oz and 6 lb 11 oz)

pollack (having good eyesight) see defects in the design of the lures and know something is wrong. With the fading light, all it sees is a fleeing baitfish. So it is with bass.

Bright conditions, with no surface agitation, send the fish deep, so it's pointless spinning shallow marks or flitting a lightweight lure across the surface film. Instead, go deep to find the fish. Bad weather and coloured seas may see fish on the surface, even over shallow ground. The type of bottom over which you are fishing has a great deal to do with the water's clarity: obviously, deep, still water will be clearer than shallow, faster moving water, because of its scouring action. Deep water, say, 6 m (20 ft) or so over a sandy bottom, may have good light levels because the sand reflects the light back, whereas a rough, rocky bottom is non-reflective and so the water is less clear. Over sand, bass may see a silhouette when observing prey below them, so darker lures are more effective. The colours chosen for use over rough ground should tend towards lures of a lighter hue.

A selection of artificial lures used for bass

How do bass attack an artificial? I think they anticipate the path of an intended meal and intercept it much as a person with a gun leads a flying duck – a high percentage of strikes are hit from the side. But bass are quite capable of swimming upwards and from behind a baitfish, swallowing it whole. This is a question of the size of the baitfish in relation to that of the bass. My own findings suggest that a bass is easily able to swallow whole a fish a tenth of its own size.

In plug fishing, bass are hooked by the tail hook, by the tail and mid-section hook together, or sometimes by the middle hook. When you're spinning a redgill, occasionally you can feel a bass pull the tail of the eel but miss the hook. I always thought this was because the bass came up close and didn't like what it saw, but a simpler explanation is that the bass calculated its angle of interception wrong by and missed – perhaps the angler speeded up the retrieve at the wrong time. Even birds of prey can only expect a 50 per cent success rate, and probably bass are the same. I've had a few bass on spinners foul-hooked outside the mouth, probably a result of the bass attacking the middle body of the spinner – as it does so the angler feels the line tighten and strikes, pulling the hooks into the outside of the jaw.

Some thought must be given to lure size. There's little point in using a 20-cm (8-in) diving plug if the fish are hitting 5-cm (2-in) sprats on the surface. It pays to carry a range of sizes extending from tiny revolving spoon-type lures to plugs and spoons 30 cm (12 in) long, so that, again, you can 'match the hatch'.

By the end of April the sea is beginning to clear from the February and March storms and at this time bass use the rough-ground beaches to hunt crabs. None the less, they will hit a lure if confronted by the right one. One way to fish this situation is for you to don a pair of chest-waders and to wade out a few metres (if the beach is shallow) for you need a depth around 1.5 or 2 m (5 or 6 ft) for the bass to see the lure properly. I prefer to find some really snaggy ground with fair-sized boulders and a moderate depth of 2 m (6 ft) or deeper. There will probably be a little surf to contend with.

Silver tobies of 28 g (1 oz) are excellent over this type of ground – it's just a case of cast and use a steady retrieve. Don't be tempted to let the spinner rise and sink by altering your speed of return – you haven't much to play with before you snag up, and the fish will see the silver flash as the spinner goes by if it's worked nearer the surface. Redgills are very effective, but only in the deeper water. To get any casting distance out of the gill, it's necessary to fish it on a paternoster, which means the lead leads the eel during the cast. I use a 0.9 or 1.25-m (3 or 4-ft) trace to the eel and about 30 cm (1 ft) of line to the lead on a three-way swivel. Over shallow, rocky ground the lead obviously keeps bumping into rocks, spoiling the eel's action, which is also heavy on tackle (see Fig. 27).

This situation is suited to plugs, especially floaters. Your casting distance will be cut, as floating plugs obviously don't carry much weight. You tease the plug through small channels, between and around boulders, and across the flanks of weedbeds. If the plug has a vane that can be preset to give a

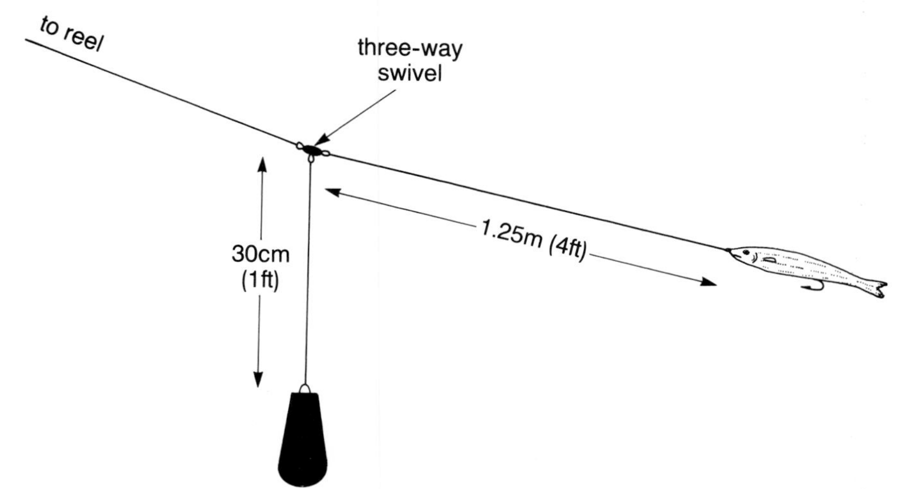

Fig. 27
Rig used when casting artificial eels from the shore

choice of depths at which to fish, then set it on its steepest setting, which makes it ride just below the surface. You can reel in a metre or so of line, then momentarily stop – allowing the plug to rise and float. Then, as you wind in again, the plug dives. This imitates a wounded fish trying to swim in short jerks.

You'll often see bass take your plug before you feel anything on the rod. Usually there's a slash on the surface as the fish hits the lure on its upward motion. Sometimes there's a boil as the fish turns away. Perhaps a flash of its silver flanks is as much pre-warning as you'll get. Bass work very close in around such boulders, and casts around 18–27 m (20–30 yd) are often enough, but again it means you must employ every scrap of available cover to hide your presence.

When a bass is hooked, it will head straight for the nearest rock or snag, so heavy but controlled pressure is needed from the start. Make sure the fish is well and truly tired before you bring it into shore. It pays, under calm, clear conditions, to walk the beach to try to find some water that holds a little more colour and suspended sediment – you'll find fish may feed here on a surface plug when the rest of the beach is dead. Deeper areas I fish with a sinking plug (preferably one with a jointed action), simply bringing it home on a steady retrieve. When a fish hits it feels as though you've snagged up, then suddenly the snag moves.

With experience you won't lose too much tackle, but if you do become snagged don't yank feverishly on the rod. Release 0.9 or 1.25 m (3 or 4 ft) of line. Then, if it's a boulder, a quick tightening of the line will often pull it free. If the plug has nosed its way into a frond of weed, give out line – often this will allow the swaying of the weed in the current to dislodge the hook. If all is fast, put the rod down, wrap the line around your fore-arm, and steadily increase the line's tension. Don't yet pull for a break, just keep the tension on and after a couple of minutes the hooks may cut through the weed. By all means, try altering the angle of the line by walking left or right, though this is not always possible on rocky beaches. Always break out using your fore-arm – never your rod, it's better to lose the plug than break your pole.

Just as in bait fishing, you'll discover little corners that fish continue to visit. These are often little bays that act as wash-ups after storms, where some current is formed as the tide crosses shallow ground, and the drop-offs where the shallows become deeper. Even the surf-line on open beaches can be covered by artificial baits. Shallow surf-strands hold good numbers of school bass and by throwing out a small redgill on a paternoster, you can enjoy some sport. Although this is a small-fish technique, bigger fish occasionally turn up. Certainly the lead being dragged across the sand doesn't seem to put the bass off and may well help them to find the eel. The same system can be used with a small, silver spinner fished solo. Look for a slight chop on the water, not mirror calm.

You can fly-fish from the surf-line, for the bass are on occasions only a few metres out. I use a reservoir trout rod with a size 8 or 9 shooting head and about 3 m (10 ft) of 4.5-kg (10-lb) test for a trace. The flies can be scrounged from a trout fisher. I recommend flies that hold some silver in their bodies, or those that have a large white wing. You can get away with a floating line over shallow sand, but for deeper marks I prefer a slow sinker.

Having cast out, slowly retrieve the fly by little tweaks, at the same time folding the line in coils in your hand or into a stripping basket around your waist. If the surf catches the line and swings it inshore just maintain contact, for it is when the fly is swept around in an arc that you often get a bite. You can trade the fly for the smallest redgill, which will be equally effective (see Fig. 28).

By fishing faster, more aerated water, you may find bigger bass more willing to take the fly. I tie my own on 2/0 hooks using goat's hair, maribou herl, white feathers, and silver tinsel. Put a fly in fast water and it really becomes alive, twisting and turning as the water rushes by. A fly-hooked bass puts up more of a fight than a fish caught in any other way.

Shallow rubbly reefs at the heads of estuaries will hold shoals of small bass over the hour either side of high water, and small silver tobies or krills will again produce the goods on very light spinning outfits and 1.8-kg (4-lb) line. When the schoolies disappear, it pays to change to a larger version and stronger line as the adults may well be around. Small American fly plugs and standard flies, on fly-rod gear, are good for this.

July and August are the main months for the use of artificials. At this time in the mouths of estuaries, huge shoals of sizeable bass will mass together. Redgills cast uptide and slowly retrieved across the tidal current can be very effective. Then fish are mostly in the surface layers, no more than 2.5–3 m (8–10 ft) down, so, to ensure that your eel is on the surface, engage the reel and begin to rewind just before it touches the water.

Weed can be a problem in estuaries, because the treble hooks snag everything they pass. The trouble can be avoided to some extent by using a paternoster and a very long trace – the lead then hits the weed first. The ideal time to fish a mark like this is during the main hours of the flood when the push is strong. Bites usually cease as the flow subsides. Other marks to spin are around harbours where little fish are common and big bass may shelter in the shadows of boat hulls, around jetties and pier footings where bass chase little pollack and sand-eels, and around any other man-made structures that hold small shoals of baitfish.

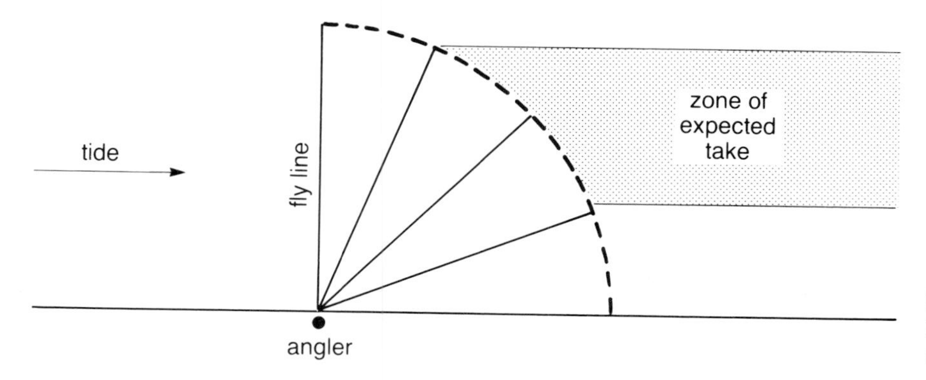

Fig. 28
Fly-fishing – zone of expected take

Rocky headlands that jut out into the tidal path and rocky groynes and breakwaters are good venues. You can walk right out to the point and drop your spinner plug or sand-eel into the tide race on the downtide side of the structure and let the tide carry the lure away for 100 m (100 yd) or so, then slowly retrieve. Bass search this type of tide run for small fish that are caught by the force of water – it's easy pickings (see Fig. 29). Cliff marks over deep water within casting range of small offshore reefs and tide runs are killing grounds for the bass. At times in such areas, the water for several hundred metres is alive with bass slashing wildly in a feeding frenzy.

It's always worth working a large spinner directly underneath the mackerel shoals that run the shoreline on hot, humid nights in July and August, for bass often work underneath these shoals, picking off dead and dying mackerel and baitfish as they fall to the ocean floor. Choose slim well-balanced plugs that don't fight the air during the cast – this can, on small multipliers, cause overruns. Check the swivel mountings on the cheaper plugs, as these can pull out on striking a good fish. Replace the hook supplied with a redgill for a Mustad pattern number 79515, as the bigger hook supplied doesn't always sink past the barb.

For night fishing there needs to be some rethinking done on the design of plugs. It's no good simply relying on the vibration caused by a wriggling lure. My own thoughts suggest that plugs with holes drilled through them and with large vanes cause air bubbles to be formed as the lure cuts its wake. This creates vibration in the water and makes the plug audible. Perhaps it also gives the bass the illusion of phosphorescence and indicates the presence of plankton. Some plugs of this sort have proved effective even on oily black nights, with no town lights near at hand to illuminate the sky.

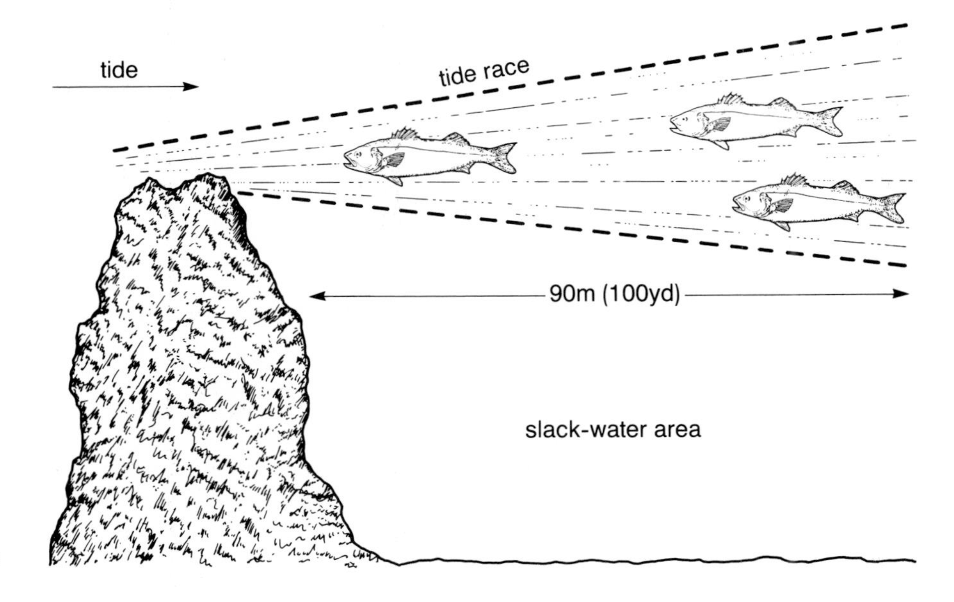

Fig. 29
Tide-race structure

8 Specimen Fish

For many years the word specimen was used for bass weighing over 4.5 kg (10 lb). Any anglers fortunate enough to haul one of these beauties ashore or across the gunnels of a boat can certainly feel justly proud of the achievement, but in reality few people catch bass weighing more than 2.7 kg (6 lb) or certainly not with any regularity. There are many reasons for this, the principal one being that the habits of bass in the middle range of 0.9–2.7 g (2–6 lb) are different from those of fish above that weight. Most anglers fail simply because they don't work hard enough and don't know enough. To catch big fish you need many skills and virtues, the chief among them being patience, attention to detail, powers of observation, casting ability, and real determination.

Big fish can and do turn up at almost any time, day or night, at any venue. So the very next bite could be the fish of your lifetime. But that is simply to rely on luck. For success we need a more rational approach.

A big fish needs a lot of food. So we need to concentrate or areas of high food output. One of the best areas to start on is the estuary. Large adults won't hang around. Once there's enough water depth to get them over the bar they'll be away. And they make the most of their time – they make a beeline for the best feeding place, using their superior power and physique to swim beyond the capabilities of the smaller fish and then letting the tide carry them to the junction of freshwater and seawater. Here there is an abundance of eels and small flatfish, sometimes even a few small coarse fish. These large fish won't stay long once the ebb gets under way, though they drop back a little slower than their smaller cousins. They will investigate, though, all the hot-spots described in Chapter 5, Estuaries, pages 53–61.

Around late April and again in September, large fish can be seen in the estuary mouths feeding heavily on small seatrout and salmon as they make their way to and from the sea. Try ledgering a large chunk of trout. Small fish can be used whole, but score the flanks with a knife to release some of the scent. Better still, cut through the whole body of a larger trout and use either a chunk with the guts still inside or the head and tail section. When using large fish baits, give the fish time to take the bait into its mouth – big bass will play with a good mouthful for several minutes before accepting it.

Some individual bass seem preoccupied with one food form. I first noticed this a few years ago when boat fishing the mouth of a west Wales estuary. We had peeler for bait and, though the tide was favourable, there were no bites. I'd seen a few tope tailing earlier on and thought that these

Stomach contents of a bass taken on a redgill – note only sand-eels are present

might be responsible for the bass's absence, so I impaled a small flounder on a large hook. I set up a long trace on a 9-kg (20-lb) outfit and slowly released the line to the out-flowing current. With the bait perhaps 73 m (80 yd) away, the tension on the line changed. I thought that a tope must have picked up the flounder and moved towards me. Windng down on the fish I felt a satisfying resistance, but knew straightaway that this was no tope – it was a hard-fighting fish that used the river current to good effect. It turned out to be a nice bass of 3.75 kg (8¼ lb). A little later I hooked one of just over 2.7 kg (6 lb). By now my friend was in action, taking fish of between 0.9 and 1.8 kg (2 and 4 lb), all on the peeler. We took two fish each for the table and I couldn't wait to gut them, for I knew the stomach contents would be of value. The first fish had eaten shore crabs and one sand-eel; the second, a small swimming crab, a shore crab, and a few shrimps; the third (the 2.7-kg fish), three small flounders; and the last (the 3.75-kg fish), four flounders and a dab. Since then I've found time and time again that one or two of the bigger fish have been taking the flounder while slightly smaller fish have preferred peeler.

When on the boat I use a lightish lead and trot the flattie away on a longish trace. From the shore I still favour a long trace but fasten the bait just above the lead on a bait-clip. The long trace is used to encourage the dead flounder to roll in the tide, for it's the flashing of its white belly that alerts the bass to a meal. I also slash the sides of the fish and cut through around the vent to introduce some blood into the water. Chunks of flounder or even halves are also good, but leave the guts hanging to encourage scent.

Moving away from estuaries, I find that open beaches rarely produce fish of above-average size. Your only chance is to fish in very rough weather and heavy surf, for, despite what many anglers say, it has to be a mighty sea before bass will move offshore. Try two rods, one out as far as you can hit it and the other close in. Peeler or mackerel make the best baits, though king ragworm is worth trying. The deeper beaches, such as Chesil Beach in Dorset and Dungeness in Kent, throw up good fish in the autumn. Use only big baits and aim to place them where the shingle of the rising bank meets the level sand of the sea bottom, for it's here the majority of the food will collect (see Fig. 30).

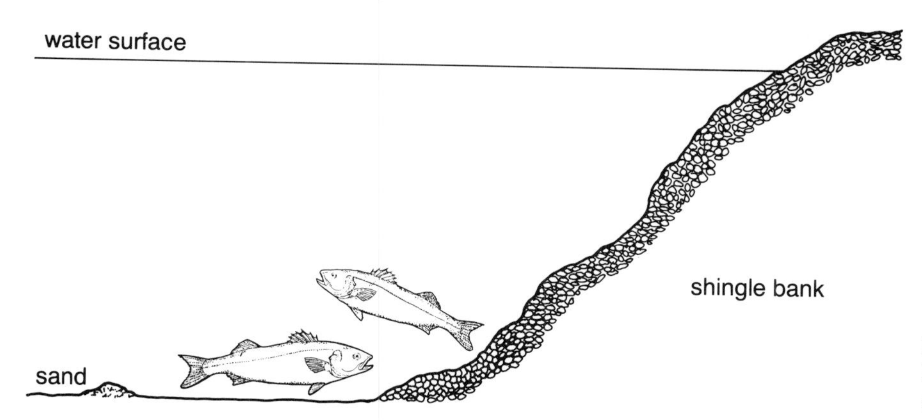

Fig. 30
Position of fish on steep to beach

These same beaches in the height of summer see mackerel herding fry close inshore. At such times it pays to use a light rod to capture a live joey and ledger this directly underneath the feeding shoal of mackerel, for big bass are fond of taking up station here and feeding on the stragglers. Again, use the lightest lead that will get the bait down on the sea bed and hold it there.

Piers and jetties hold their share of good fish. A dead or live bait works best. Use the following rig: with your reel line threaded through the rings slide one eye of a swivel on to the line so that it slides freely; tie directly to the reel line a second swivel, large enough in the eye to halt the upper swivel; to the bottom eye of the second swivel tie 1.8–3 m (6–10 ft) of line and add the lead; to the first swivel tie a trace around 1.8 m (6 ft) in length and add your hook and bait (see Fig. 31).

Hold on to the bait while you cast out the lead, or drop it over the side. Then when the lead is down, let the bait slide down the line. If you hold your rod you should be able to feel the bait become agitated as a big fish makes it presence felt. Bites are usually fairly savage affairs. This method only works effectively where you have depth and height to allow a steep trajectory of line. Some deep-rock marks also respond favourably to this trick.

Tide races off rocky headlands hold bass of good size, but you must fish much deeper. Only smaller fish will be present in the upper layers. The big fish go very deep, where the debris from the dead and dying baitfish shoals will fall in their path. They usually stay well downtide of the smaller fish.

Finding large fish on rough-ground beaches is not easy. There is so much food everywhere that the main food areas are difficult to locate. Try to find a well-stocked area with easy and deepish access to the open sea through the low-tide mark. Pebbly gullies, or the edge of rocky reefs where the tide has dug the sand and shale away, are good places. If you notice a deep hole among shallower ground that the tide burns through, then that is a good place to try.

Certain areas keep producing the specimens, and always on the same size of tides. Almost everywhere in the country big bass and middle-sized tides go together. There are exceptions, but my records, kept over a few years, show that tides between 7.9 and 8.5 (26 and 28 ft) on the Liverpool Scale turned up over 70 per cent of the big fish. It doesn't matter if the weather is rough; it's at this time that most of the bass's food is washed out of their holes.

Large pieces of peeler crab are fine early in the season, but use big baits – say three or four middling crabs well smashed-up and bound on to a 7/0

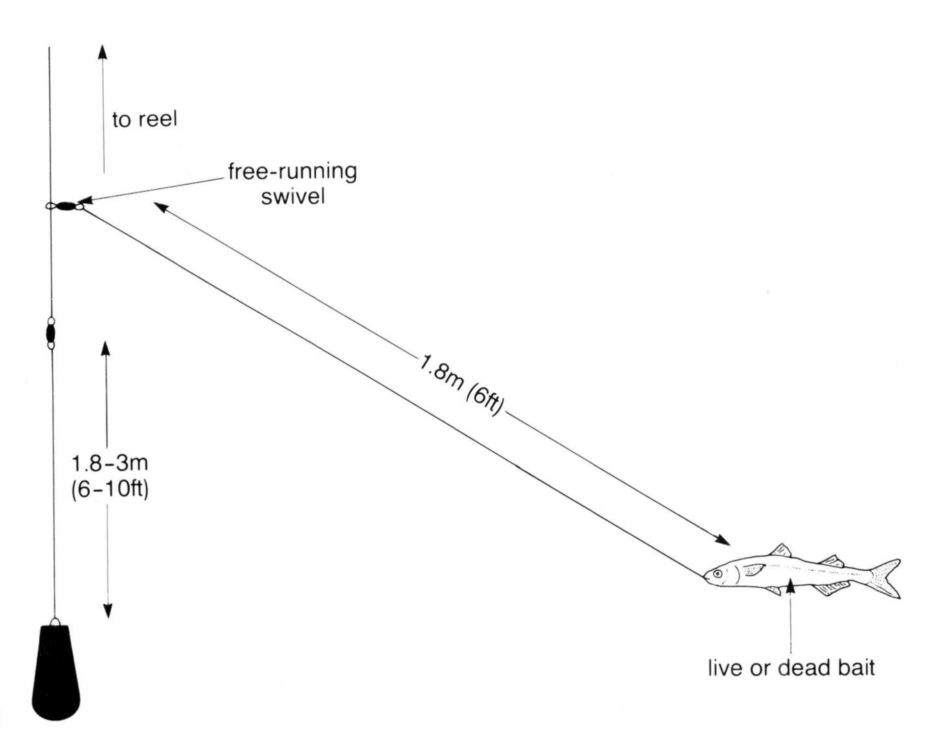

Fig. 31
Live or dead bait rig

long-shanked Aberdeen. I seem to do best with a slightly longer trace than normal.

If you can find a rock drop-off into a main tidal current on to sand or shingle, or even a kelp bed this long, flowing trace baited with crab, lug, or rag will work well. It has proved very effective in the Menai Straits in North Wales, which consists mainly of marks of this sort throughout its length.

During the summer, most big fish will shoal up with all the other bass, preying on sprat and sand-eel shoals, but a few of the bigger fish stay on the inshore marks. Don't neglect your standard marks if time and tide suggest you should fish.

By late August the fish will move inshore and though standard shore-peeler baits and even half or whole mackerel will be taken, you increase your chances by three if you bait up with edible peeler. This will fish right through until the bass leave in October.

It often strikes me that fish are not given enough respect for their intelligence. They are wise in the environment in which they live. Big fish have a great deal of experience; they may well have been hooked and lost, or at least pricked by a hook on the strike, so when feeding on the bottom they are naturally cautious. They are also solitary fish; they have time to decide whether or not to take that succulent piece of peeler without worrying that a rival will snatch it from them.

Most of the big fish that move inshore during autumn are used to eating food on the hoof, so to speak; normally their prey is making a run for it. How often do they come across a large lump of crabmeat sitting unmoving on the sea bed? Not very often, I would have thought.

Small baits are sometimes surprisingly successful at catching big fish. Perhaps the smaller the bait the more natural it looks – which could go some way to explaining the success beginners sometimes have when using small baits for flatfish and the like. Less convincing is the theory that the small bait attracts small fish that in turn attract the big fish.

I have used small baits on light lines in areas that I know hold good bass and the results have been encouraging. (By small baits I mean enough crab to fill a size 1/0 hook or half a medium-size lug.) The main problem is that really big fish like the roughest, snaggiest ground they can find, which defeats the light-tackle rod logic. It's a different proposition if you can ambush them *en route* to their feeding grounds.

What sort of bite can you expect? Well, you can certainly expect the unexpected. Fish differ in the way that they will take the bait. Most bites will be very tentative – you may feel nothing definite through the rod, simply sensing that something is afoot. A few minutes may elapse before you see your rod tip crash down as the fish powers away. Another classic, especially on crab, is a faint but discernible single 'tap', just as if a little piece of weed fondled the line before the tide carried it on. How to deal with strikes like these is set out on pages 36–37.

Some big bass will pick up bait in their lips and shake it like a dog. I can think of no good reason for this, unless the bass thinks the crab is still alive and is trying to kill it. But why bother? This behaviour produces a really weird feeling through the rod and hook-ups on the strike are only mediocre. Some fish hit so hard that the rod is yanked seawards with such force that the angler may be overbalanced. These fish usually hook themselves. You'll have a few slack liners that pick the bait up and move inshore. Some big bass imitate little flounders and just gently rattle the rod tip. I tend to hit these bites quickly for a big fish will have the hook in its mouth and delay only gives it time to spit out the bait. Look out for the fish that sucks the bait into its mouth and then blows it out again two or three times in succession. The only advice I can offer is to hit when your instinct tells you it's right. Finally, there is the bass that runs a few metres with the bait and then drops it. That fish usually doesn't return to the bait. Some do, though, and I release a little line again and wait for the fish to pull the line tight before striking.

The kind of fight a monster will put up depends largely on its surroundings. If there are snags within easy reach the big bass will go for them in one awe-inspiring run. It's imperative to halt it before it gets there or the fish is certainly lost. When it's turned it will rest for a few seconds then choose a new target. After two or three of these runs things will quieten down and the fish will simply kite around. But expect a further powerful run when the fish catches sight of you. Over shallow sandy beaches and estuaries the pattern is much the same – a good run or two with the odd lunge in between. Expect fireworks when you draw the fish into the surf.

A fish hooked in a fast current will dive to the bottom and shake its head. Be on your guard against fast unstoppable runs when you draw it near the surface. Some fish will swim towards you, making you think the hook hold has been broken. If you're in a boat, with some depth below, there'll be plenty of head-shaking and downward lunges, but the only real run of the contest is likely to be when the fish sees the hull. Some try to get underneath the hull, so watch out for that.

A fish played against a fast-moving tide run may well have the habit of increasing water resistance by opening its mouth, thus increasing the resistance of the water against it. If this happens, I find that dropping the rod to one side and altering the angle of pull makes the mouth close.

Big fish can turn up at any time, but I favour an ebbing tide with some colour in the water in the evenings or, for peak confidence, a low water that coincides with the first flush of the dawn. The best period is always from late August until early November. I think big bass hang around and feed on the first of the inshore whiting, before moving off as the inshore temperature drops. The biggest bass have a habit of showing when the fishing has been poor for a period of some days, which could be, as I've said, because there's then little competition for food.

I have noted before that small bass do not feed together with medium bass, but there is another divide – that between big bass and very big bass. These old adults are to a certain extent territorial – they'll return to the same feeding grounds year after year and must defend their ground to some extent. They return to their feeding grounds each year with precision timing – within a few days of the same date and on the same set of tidal heights. They will have, though, different areas for different seasons – one for spring, one (offshore around a particular reef) for the summer, and one (inshore) for autumn. It's safe to assume they leave around the same time each year, though this may be governed more by the water temperature than by the date.

Bass are quite willing to devour their own kind (another reason for non-mixing) and several large fish I've gutted have contained small school fish up to about 0.25 kg ($\frac{1}{2}$ lb). The little bass are always swallowed head first to avoid the sharp dorsal spines doing damage. Mullet are eaten with fair regularity. I've yet to feel the need to use mullet for bait, but it's one the big-fish angler shouldn't ignore. Likewise, squid used whole is responsible for many fine captures, though you wait a long time for a bite.

The most important factor in catching big fish is the amount of time you put in. The more hours you fish, the better chance you have of taking a lunker. The rule is simple – put in the most hours at the most likely times at the most likely places.

9 Strategy and Confidence

Any project in life needs careful thought before any attempt at commitment is made and the same applies to angling. It's no good going bass *fishing* in name only. Get one important factor wrong and you blank.

To be consistent on a regular basis takes work, study, and observation. In the beginning you won't catch much, but as the seasons pass and you acquire real knowledge so your score of fish will increase. There's much truth in the old saying that 90 per cent of the fish are caught by 10 per cent of the anglers. The successful 10 per cent are those who think about the problems they encounter and, through sheer hard graft and many mistakes, come up with a solution.

RECORDS AND SOURCES OF INFORMATION

Get into the habit of keeping a diary – every time you wet a line record it as soon as you return home, while all is fresh in your memory. The minimum information to record is as follows: state of the tide, tide height, kind of tide (neap or spring), wind direction and force, state of sea (rough or calm), clarity of water, cloud cover, exact time fished, time at which bites started and ceased, fish caught, distance cast, how many bites missed, and stomach contents of any fish killed. It is useful to record your impressions of how the session went, along with any other relevant observations. From recording such details for each separate mark over a few seasons you will begin to see patterns emerge – a particular height of tide or a due westerly may prove excellent at mark A while at mark B you'll sit there all night for nothing. A diary not only enables you to put yourself on to fish under the best conditions, but also avoids wasted effort.

Keep a file of cuttings or make notes from the weekly pages of angling magazines and papers that record the venues from where big fish or good catches have come. I would never suggest that you hare off to these venues, rod in hand, in the vain hope of cashing in on others' good fortune, for chasing fish rarely works. It's far better to wait until the next set of big spring tides, when the ground over which these fish were taken can be clearly viewed at low water. Leave your rod at home for this. It always pays to study these areas carefully so that you can recognise the places where fish are likely to feed when you fish the mark yourself. I'd go so far as to say that if you need to fish other anglers' marks to find fish, then you'll never quite make the grade as a thinking bass angler.

I use my camera to record – in colour – the detail of the beach, and in this way notice the small changes that can happen through the winter storms. If the marks you wish to fish aren't uncovered on the big tides, use the advantage of high ground on calm sunny days to spot sand patches amongst the rock, weedbeds, and deeper gullies that the fish may feed in. If this luxury is even denied you, a trip to your local quay may turn up some information from commercial fishermen who, providing you're polite, may pass on the odd tip or two. A better system still is to get to know retired commercial fishermen. If you track them down to their local watering hole they may pass on some of their knowledge now that their living no longer depends on it.

A good source of information is the local sub-aqua club, whose members may be willing to go down and map the place in question for you on one of their exercises. This on-the-spot observation is worth a hundred rumours. I once spent a full spring looking for a group of rocks surrounded by sand some 275 m (300 yds) offshore on the third-hand advice of an acquaintance. I eventually found it, certainly 275 m (300 yd) offshore, but two-and-a-half miles to the south west.

Always treat hearsay catches with scepticism, for fish do tend to grow with every conversation. If somebody says they had bass last night of 1 or 2 kg (or 3, 4, and 5 lb) there could be something amiss. If, on the other hand, you hear of fish weighing 1.75 or 2.5 kg (or 3 lb 12 oz, 4 lb 3 oz, and 5 lb 9 oz), these could well be fact – for the addition of the decimal point or ounces usually signifies some truth.

There's nothing wrong with telling a good friend about a productive mark you've just discovered, but it's folly to broadcast it to all and sundry, because the very next day there won't be room for you – all the space will have been taken. It's often necessary to use as little light as you can manage with, so as not to advertise the position you are fishing. Tilley and other pressure lamps are not suitable in most cases.

BAIT

Never go fishing with second-class bait for you'll achieve second-class results. When low water is at 3.30 a.m. and it's the only tide on which you can collect crabs because of work commitments, most people wouldn't bother – but it's those who do and still put a full day's work in that will enjoy the most reward. Even good, reliable tackle shops that sell live bait cannot always be depended upon. Bear this in mind, and when you've collected your bait look after it – keep it cool and lively.

I've always set great store by putting a fresh, smelly bait in the water to help the fish find it more easily, and the idea of extra ground bait always appealed to me, but my efforts have produced nothing of significance. First

I crushed some hardback crabs and put them in a fine-meshed bag, and left this in a place where the scent would waft through a potential feeding area, but little happened. I even tried injecting my crab baits with amino-acids as extra stimulant, and with emulsifiers to break up the scent trail more quickly, but again I remain to be convinced. One thing did occur to me, and that was that a single, strong scent may well be followed by a hunting bass, but a wider, weaker scent could well be left alone. A scent split into avenues by boulders and the like could also confuse the fish.

THE WEATHER

I set great store by the weather, and suggest you acquire at least a basic understanding of how lows and highs and the changing seasons manifest themselves – for it's these factors that dictate more than anything the availability of fish on a national and local scale. To understand the weather you need little more than a television set and good powers of observation, though a barometer can help you recognise problems more quickly.

Gales with winds over Force 8, coming in from the Atlantic, are shown on the barometer by the needle falling, the wind backing in an anti-clockwise direction. Similarly, a rapidly rising needle occurs when the wind is veering in a clockwise direction. You can usually spot this 48 hours before the gale arrives, though it can vary in different parts of the country. Southerly gales in Britain usually show as a falling barometer, whilst north-westerlies appear as a rising needle. These observations are associated with the south and west coasts of Britain, where most bassing is done.

If winds have been persistently westerly, with bands of alternatively good and bad weather followed by a falling barometer, the wind will veer south-west, going back to the west before becoming north-westerly later. By watching the television weather forecasts and noting the weather charts you can spot a low forming over the eastern seaboard of the United States and track it as it moves across the Atlantic in a progressively eastern direction, deepening all the time. Should a ridge of high pressure be evident around British shores, these lows are forced north, usually moving above Scotland, giving fine settled weather. If no high pressure intervenes, the low advances roughly through the middle of the British Isles. To the south of these lows you can expect first southerly, followed by south-westerly, then westerly and finally north-westerly winds. To the north of the depression, you'll have south-east, going east through north-east winds. Extensive high-pressure areas have a habit of taking up station over the USSR giving Britain and Northern Europe prolonged easterly winds. These often die away to the south-east but at dawn may reach gusts of Force 6.

At times of high pressure dominant over Britain, tides may advance a little further up the tideline than anticipated, and by the same token ebb out a little further. In periods of low pressure and conflicting winds, tides may fall short of their intended target. It pays to note such things when wading to offshore estuary bars, and so on, and the same applies during storm conditions, when tides can be higher than anticipated.

Anglers who live close to the sea soon note how slack water at low and high tides brings a change in the weather. It's caused by the changing water currents out to sea, which are themselves partly responsible for creating wind currents. A bank of low pressure may be held offshore by an ebbing tide, only to race shorewards as the flood gets underway. Strong onshore winds ease off in the main as the flood dies and the ebb begins to flow strongly. Rain may cease or start, drizzle can disappear or become a downpour. Such fluctuations in temperature – though relatively small – are easily felt by us at such times.

In periods of heavy gales weed often makes fishing a chore rather than a pleasure, but by reading the wind and tidal currents you should be able to choose a venue that helps you avoid the worst of the menace. Weed is always pushed along in a line that lies straight with the wind. Tidal flow has much less to do with weed deposition than most people realise. Any tidal influence usually shows as a slightly sideways drift. By finding little corners at the ends of beaches or small coves that face directly away from the prevailing wind, weed deposits should be light or non-existent. At the other end of the beach, where the wind has blown the weed, there may be huge banks of the stuff, 0.6 or 0.9 m (2 or 3 ft) high, depending on the severity and duration of the storm. Fishing would obviously be impossible here.

Gales that pass directly over the area you wish to fish may prove beneficial, for in the eye of the storm or the inner core surrounded by strong winds all will be calm. Whilst the sea is violent, crashing with huge rollers, for a few hours you may enjoy a period of flat calm, enabling you to cast far out beyond the storm-tossed waters to where the occasional bass may be feeding.

On surf beaches you can often see a demarcation line of sand suspended as sandy-brown water before you reach the deep green of the proper settled sea. Put a bait in at this junction and you could do well. The majority of beaches fish in accordance with the way the wind strikes them: a direct wind that blows the beach full in its face gives high solid surf, yet if the wind is at even the slightest angle from either side the effect is much less. As bass prefer rough water, onshore winds will always be the best, though some beaches or even parts of the same beach may differ as a much more mitigating influence, such as a food-carrying current, takes over.

Too many people laugh at old sayings such as 'red sky at night, shepherds delight'. What they fail to realise is that these are based on observations built up over many centuries. They are very accurate and can foretell a change often before the weather office does. There are hundreds of such sayings, yet only a few are relevant to the angler. The following are well worth noting.

'When the wind's in the east, it's there for three days at least'. This saying is based on those high pressures that sit over Russia, often present virtually unchanged for nine or ten days and giving those solid easterlies. High barometric pressure is rarely associated with good catches. At such times have a look at commercial-catch reports – even the trawlers and netters do badly. This is because of a combination of barometric pressure, calm, clear seas, and little surf movement. Anglers change the words of this saying to 'When the wind's in the east, the fish bite the least'. To a certain extent, on the east coast of England the opposite applies: there the east wind is onshore, though even here I've never done well under a direct easterly. For the first few tides after the wind has gone into the east, the fishing may not be too bad, but as the effects of the easterly wind are slowly felt, further tides are less likely to produce good results.

'When the wind's in the north, the skilful fisher goes not forth'. The north wind is another that is allied to high pressure, although not quite as severe as the easterly for producing poor fishing, but still far from good for most types of bassing. 'When the wind's in the south, it blows the bait in the fish's mouth'. This wind is not quite as good as the westerly, but as the words imply, it's an excellent fishing wind, being the companion to a low-pressure system. Any beach that receives a reasonable degree of directness from this wind will be good. 'When the wind's in the west, the fish bite the best'. Three-quarters southwest west and northwest are all excellent when they are applying themselves to the right venues, for all are low-pressure winds that encourage bass to feed.

Strong, clearly-defined sunsets give hints of a fine day to follow. Small patches of wispy cloud which may appear on the horizon even after a totally cloudless day, termed 'sunset cloud', are not associated with the coming of poor weather, as some believe. Pale, watery sunsets foretell rain. If you observe prisms of rainbow colours around the setting sun, you can bank on rain to follow.

The composition and formation of clouds can tell us a great deal about forthcoming weather patterns, and it's not difficult to learn and recognise a few of these signs. You can concentrate on three basic types: obviously, storm clouds, then clouds holding numerous showers and finally fine-weather clouds.

The nimbus is the low-level, heavy-grey cloud that envelops the sky, blotting out much of the light, and giving periods of heavy rain. As this cloud approaches, any high, thin-in-composition cloud that lies in all directions above the nimbus suggests that rain will be prolonged and heavy. If little or none of the higher, thin cloud is evident, then the rainfall will be short. Clearing nimbus cloud, followed by roughly defined cloud that increases in volume, indicates that the wind will also increase. Dissipating cloud indicates that the winds will gradually fall away.

Cumulus or thunder clouds stand erect in tall columns with sharp edges, and have a bronzy-coloured tinge. In other words, they look angry. Shower cumulus stand like the sky-scrapers of New York, reaching upwards from wide foundations that increase to cover the sky by late evening. Squalls are synonymous with these formations.

Any cloud build-up during the day, from a clear-blue morning sky increasing in cloud intensity towards evening, promises a change for the worst. Cirro-cumulus or mackerel skies – small, blotchy clouds of a feathery shape very high in the sky during settled periods – foretell a change to unsettled weather with worse to come. There's a sailors' rhyme for this: 'Mackerel skies and mare's tails, make tall ships carry short sails'. Watch this cloud, for if it loses height and thickens quickly rain is on the way. Winds will come from the direction in which the mare's tails are travelling, and they are likely to be strong.

After a good period of calm weather, quickening clouds mean a change is on the way. The same applies when very high, fine cloud develops – a gradual change to wet weather is on the way. Soft, gentle clouds can be considered fair-weather clouds, and hard, clearly-defined clouds are impending storm clouds.

'Seagull, seagull, sit on the sand, there's no fine weather when you're on the land.' This saying predicts strong winds, for the seagull senses the change in barometric pressure and sits on the beach to offer the least resistance to the increasing wind. Incidentally, I've noticed that the seagull, when sitting in such a way, always faces the oncoming wind. 'Rain before seven, fine by eleven'. Basically, this saying means that if you wake up to rain, by mid-morning it may well have cleared, as the front will have passed over. If it starts to rain after 8 a.m., forget the barbecue – it's likely to rain all day. Smoke rising from a chimney only to dip down in a crescent to caress the roof tiles denotes poor weather to follow. If, however, the smoke travels straight up, fine weather will be the order of the day.

THE SEA

The sea itself holds many clues to help us decide when to fish. During periods of high pressure a flat sea may suddenly show an increase in activity, a good ground swell becoming evident. This is because of a storm and high winds perhaps several hundred miles away. These conditions are well worth fishing.

The sea will have a different colour when the wind is in a certain direction. On my own part of the Welsh coast, a northerly wind that holds for several days colours the sea a definite black and all fishing is poor. I think this is as a result of cold water being pushed down from the north through the Irish sea. Warm water is usually a light green or blue, perhaps tinted by the plankton swimming in the upper layers. Another give-away for warmer water is the presence of jellyfish. Find jellyfish and invariably you'll find mackerel. If fresh jellyfish are washing up on the beach, then fish – bass – are likely to be present. Good catches often come at such times.

Too many anglers fish by the tides, never fully comprehending the tide's influences on the fish and seashore environment. Tides are the result of gravitational pull, mainly from the moon but also to a lesser extent from the sun. The moon's pull is a horizontal one. As the moon follows its arc-shaped path in the sky, so the water is pulled after it. Take note when you're on the beach at the time of the full moon and when the sky is clear: you'll see that as the moon reaches the height of its arc, the tides begin to ebb.

The moon orbits the earth once every 28 days, but the earth rotates more quickly – as we all know, once in every 24 hours. The pull of the moon on the world's water, coupled with the constant rotation of the earth, produces a wedge of water or tidal wave. This is unnoticeable out in the ocean proper, but on approaching the land-mass its velocity is reduced while its height increases. The same principle applies when surf builds up on a beach of shallowing sand.

This wedge of water flows on in an eastwards course across the Altantic, hitting the south and west coasts of Ireland and, at roughly the same time, the coast of Cornwall. It gives high tides at the same hour. The land-mass deflects streams of water up the Irish Sea and into the English Channel, giving different high-tide times the further it travels. Each day has two high-tide times, one when the moon is directly overhead and the other when it is on the other side of the earth. Because of the 24-hour rotation of the earth, the moon, travelling on its 28-day lunar orbit, arrives at the same point (on average) 50 minutes later each day. This time difference is less on spring tides and more on neap tides. When the sun and moon combine in their gravitational pull, we experience the biggest tides of the month. The less these two forces work together, the weaker the tide. Spring tides occur roughly two days after the new and full moons. When the sun and moon are on the same side of the planet, we have the new moon, but when the full moon is up, the moon and sun are on opposite sides.

There is also an annual cycle, around the spring and autumn equinoxes, approximately 21 March and 21 September. At these times the pull of the moon and sun is in its most direct line, giving the biggest tides of the year. This is most obvious on beaches that experience fast lateral tide runs. These are at their strongest when water is on the move during the spring tides, but the effect is however, much less evident on the neap tides. On a rising tide, the percentage of water movement is as follows: 25 per cent in the first two hours, 50 per cent in the middle two, and 25 per cent in the last two hours of the flood, the ebb being identical.

CONFIDENCE

We all endure days when things never seem to go right. Usually we feel less than 100 per cent though we're not actually ill. There's no real explanation for this, but our body-clock seems a little off balance. What could have happened is a partial lapse in concentration – our mind has strayed from the job in hand. We were probably unaware of something going awry in something we do as a matter of course, but from then on our mind or subconcious keeps reverting back to this initial upset, and the whole day becomes a long chain of misdemeanours.

What has all this to do with fishing? Well, take, for example, any bassing trip. You get to your mark on time, your bait is good, you go through the ritual of sharpening the hook and double checking your knots. The cast is made and you settle down with rod in hand to await the bites you know will come at a certain time – but they don't. You start to fidget, and your mind keeps asking the same questions: 'Where are they?' 'Should I have gone to mark B?' 'Is my presentation all it should be?' Generally, you work yourself into such a state that by the time a bite does ensue, you couldn't hit a barn door because your temperament is completely wrong.

It's confidence that counts. Hit the first bite or send the sinker out past the 100-m (120-yd) band with your first cast, and you'll feel as if you could hit the moon. Your confidence soars, and so do your catches. Confidence comes from knowing you've done things in the right order – which is why you should keep a diary, make sure the bait is fresh, the tackle in first-class working order, and so on.

You can avoid the more obvious upsets by getting into a routine. Pack your tackle the night before, when your mind is clear, and you won't forget anything. Check your reels and rods. Make your decision about which venue to fish in accordance with the prevailing weather forecast – don't hum and haw between two or three different venues until the last minute, for you'll choose the wrong one. Selection must be on merit alone. Set off in plenty of time – if you suffer a puncture you'll then have plenty of time to change the tyre without missing out on the fishing. Some anglers key themselves up to fish one particular spot. If someone else has beaten them to it, then the whole night falls apart. This is one time when an alternative mark pays off.

By continually holding the rod you learn to interpret the messages the line imparts to your hands: that gentle pluck felt like a piece of weed brushing the line. You come to recognise the particular sensation regular bassers get that lets them know, a few seconds before a bite comes, that a bass is interested. It's like a sixth sense – a feeling that comes over you – and it becomes reliable. When you've something on your mind, these feelings are obscured, and the realisation you've just had a bite takes longer to dawn. In other words, your reaction time is slower. After this happens you usually become worked up, holding the rod in the prone pre-strike position until your arms ache. The slightest movement you feel is struck savagely and too quickly. You're now so confused that the whole situation becomes ridiculous.

On some trips, you know as soon as you set foot on the beach or rocks that you will catch. There's nothing clairvoyant in this. What probably happens is that your natural senses come into play. They've weighed up past experiences and conditions and, like a computer, when all this information is deciphered the right answer comes out. When you have this feeling – and hit the first bite with a well-hooked fish – your adrenalin starts to flow and all your senses come alive. You hit peak form. This is a combination of good mental attitude, increased adrenalin flow, and high levels of confidence. It's part of the reason some anglers experience runs, when they can't put a foot wrong. It's all down to confidence that's inspired by the right technique.

Poor bait and problems with tackle instil bad confidence and as a result catches fall. We've all had nights when we've said 'I shan't do any good tonight'. Though the rod goes thumping over to a good bite, we clean miss it. We've already convinced ourselves we'll blank – and we do. Keep your lucky charm safe and don't forget it. Just worrying about it will make you fish badly. Make every effort to have a clear conscience.

It's rare to find a fishing mate who has the same values as yourself (usually they turn up late and the best part of the tide is missed). Learn to enjoy your own company – your organisation will be better and there are fewer distractions. If you must fish in groups, don't worry about looking a fool if you crack off or whatever. If you think it you'll do it. It always pays to separate yourself 45 m (50 yd) or so. If you're lucky enough to have like-minded friends, so much the better. If not, fish alone.

Your own character make-up will tell you about your potential abilities as an angler. If, for instance, you're one of those who tie a suspect knot and say 'it'll do' , you're in trouble, If the alarm goes off a 3.30 a.m. for you to catch low water at 4.30 a.m. and you say to yourself 'forget it, I'll go tomorrow', your potential is limited. You'll have noticed that it's the same people who are always on the scrounge for tackle and bait, who always turn up late and winge at the first raindrop. If you fall into this category don't take up bassing as a serious pastime. Time and time again, it's the anglers who bother who bring home the lunkers.

To sum up: create a sound platform of knowlege to enable you to catch. Stick with the same preparatory routines and rituals. Assess the best marks and bait. The end result of all this is a consistent attitude that almost wills the fish to consume the bait and hidden hook – what some anglers call 'luck'.

10 Tackle for Bass

As today's tackle will, through the quickening speed of development, be out of date tomorrow, it's my intention just to touch upon rod and reel choice and spend more time on the traces, rigs, and so on, that have a real influence on whether we catch fish or not.

RODS

Before any purchase of rod is made, it's important to decide into which category of angling – (rock, surf beach, estuary) – the majority of trips will fall. On the other hand, if you want to diversify to a large degree, you'll need to select a model that gives at least some sport and feel. Light to middling rough can be challenged with a 3.4–3.7-m (11–12-ft) two-piece fibreglass or carbon-glass mix, aimed at casting 28–85 g (1–3 oz). A fairly fast taper aids bite detection and gives instant knowledge back to your hands. A softer rod of the same length could be considered, which will work well on the cast and keep delicate crab baits intact. These blanks have a slower taper and feel is slightly dampened. Feelings transmitted up the line on the fast taper are harsh, hard affairs, whereas on the slower taper bites are softer, less vicious in feel, due to the springiness of the blank.

These rods are both equally happy on the surf-line of clean beaches, fishing crab and lug baits out to almost the 90-m (100-yd) band, with nothing more than a simple overhead cast. Moderate surf on such places can usually be negotiated with around 85-g (3-oz) breakout leads. There's little point in using anything heavier if you don't need to.

Rougher ground, with kelp and large boulders, needs something with extra power – say a casting capability of 110 or 140 g (4 or 5 oz) with a quickish taper – but not a stiff, long-range blank that takes a great deal of body power to bend. It's important to understand that it's not extra distance we're looking for here, just the extra strength needed to combat rough ground and probably deeper, faster water. On modern designs, bite detection will still be excellent, yet you have the soft action of the blank, which is forgiving in these situations where a large fish may lunge around. Stiff rods capable of massive distances are harsh, and bend little, adding more strain to the line and increasing the risk of tearing out an otherwise secure hook hold. These middle-of-the-road rods are, of course, capable of fishing at much greater range, but to do so you must learn more efficient casting styles – about which more later.

The last category of rod is for the angler who, out of necessity, needs to fish baits well out from the shore and use big leads to hold the bait down in the fast tide run. Though the rod is equally happy lobbing 170 or 200 g (6 or 7 oz) into a sand patch at the base of a kelp-strewn rock in 6 m (20 ft) of white water, these rods are best with fast taper – the last 45 cm (18 in) or so being all fibreglass on carbon-mix rods. This is fairly soft, and aids bite detection. It also helps to smooth out the cast. The middle section is much stiffer and takes a great deal of body power to put some bend in it. The butt section is either stiff alloy or a carbon mix. These, on the hardest casts, are used as a solid lever. All the power transmitted from your body to the lead is transferred to the mid-section and the butt. Your body, on the release, is using the butt section purely as a lever. It's the power stored in the mid-section that hurls out the sinker to those huge distances.

Whichever classification of rod you choose, extra decisions have to be made. For instance, many models give you a choice of two pieces of equal sections for ease of transportation, though they may do a 2.4-m (7 ft 9-in) tip and a 1.30-m (4 ft 3-in) butt, or thereabouts. If you can live with the transport problems, go for the latter, for though many good anglers say there is no difference, ask someone who handles a rod four or five times a week – they'll invariably take the long tip and short butt. This combination has a hint more precision in both casting and bite detection.

Several other factors should be considered. Ordinary fibreglass is heavier and thicker than a carbon-glass mix. The lighter a completed rod is, the longer you can hold it, giving an increase in bite detection. However, avoid very thin butts on the lighter range, for your hand grip is fighting itself. Similarly on the beefy casting poles – an outside diameter exceeding 30 mm (1⅛ in) is too thick, and you lose power during the cast.

Still on the subject of lightness and comfort, any keen bass angler would be well advised to learn to build their own rods. Not only do you save a few pence but more importantly, you can use better products and build the blank to suit your own stance and grip. Always save weight where possible. The days of cork are long since passed, shrink tube (which decreases in diameter when exposed to heat) making an excellent covering for all butts. A simple rubber sleeve from a cricket bat where the reel goes is fine. Two coasters or jubilee clips to fix the reel, and another grip at the base and a butt pad are really all you need. This encourages that hard feel straight through to your hands, giving you instant assessment of bites. Any extra items, such as standard reel seats and soft foam grips, soften the messages your hands receive. Extra weight also dulls any feelings running up the line. Immediately you return from a trip, wash the whole rod in warm, soapy water, and then rinse. By doing this you'll prolong its service life by a couple of seasons and keep the rings in good shape.

Boat rods are really the same. For light fishing in estuaries or over ground where the tide is not too fierce, a 56–110 g (2–4-oz) uptider is good around the 3-m (10-ft) mark. In heavier water, step up to a 110–225-g (4–8-oz) model, and for trolling a standard 5.5–6.8-kg (12–15-lb) class rod is fine. If you've a good chance of a big fish hitting the bait hard, well back from the boat, a 9-kg (20-lb) class might be considered. I stipulate standard boat rods because longer spinning rods and uptiders bend too much on the strike, and so fish are often lost. For once I would choose the stiffer 2-m (7-ft) rods for ease of hooking and better trolling control.

REELS

Many people winge and moan about small bait-casters, saying they're unreliable and easily rot. If you're idle and never clean them, they do, but conscientious bassers will find them the mainstay of their armoury. Sensibly fished, they'll cope with light to middling rough, beaches, estuaries, and all ultra-long range work. Only in real rough and on boats will other choices have to be made.

Good reel models are less apt to change as frequently as rods, so we can assess some models in order that, when you make your own choice, you'll have some comparisons to draw upon. For light spinning and plug fishing, something in the size bracket of the ABU 5500c is ideal, whilst on the beach and middling rough the 6500c, by the same company, is excellent – as is the Daiwa 6HM Millionaire. Both come with level winds, though you may prefer to remove these if you need to cast long distances to reach your fish. For rougher situations and all boat work, I have no hesitation in recommending the ABU 7000c – it's the reel I use to judge all others. In the same size range, Daiwa and Penn manufacture reels of high quality in several models, as do Shimano.

Never neglect the fixed spool, which can compete on an almost equal basis with the multipliers. What the old mangle lacks, though, is finesse: you never achieve the smoothness and direct feel you achieve with the revolving spool. Don't select too big a reel for spinning and plugging, something that holds about 180 m (200 yd) of 4.5-kg (10-lb) line is about right, but for long-range work purchase the biggest model you can find and load it to the very top of the spool lip. Fixed spools cast and fish best with the finer lines under 6.8-kg (15-lb) test – over this, flow problems begin.

Multipliers respond particularly well to a procedure of careful running-in. This is best done before you actually take one fishing. Pick a clear field or deserted beach and select a middle-sized weight – 85 or 110 g (3 or 4 oz) is ideal – and cast out gently, using an overhead lob 45 m (50 yd) or so. Complete fifty casts, then put down a hundred casts to the 90-m (100-yd) mark, followed by another hundred to the 120–135-m (130–150-yd) band. By this time all the parts will have polished themselves to match each other; the reel will have a smooth, silky feel, and also an increased life span.

It pays to strip the reel thoroughly, directly after purchase, and to wash out any swarf or machine waste before relubricating properly. Don't over-tighten the drag, and never use heavy retrieve pressure directly on the gears when hauling weed or fish. Always remove salt deposits after fishing by trickling warm water over the side plates, then leave in a warm room or airing cupboard. The running-in procedure only affects the fixed spool on the retrieve, for during the cast there are no moving parts.

Line lay is controlled by the level wind on multipliers, and is mostly fine for fishing, but when casting distances in excess of 90 m (100 yd) with baits, the removal of this device is necessary to avoid frictional loss on the level wind gears, and to allow your thumb full access to the spool for lock-down on a powerful cast. Ready-modified frames are available from several tackle dealers, and for the do-it-yourself person there are kits that are easily fitted. These consist of a solid bar that fits into the two recesses left by the level wind. This should just slide in with slight pressure. If it won't, file a little away in equal amounts from each end. However after converting several models of both types I've never had one that was difficult. When the new bar is fitted, you can add a drop of Locktite or a similar substance to the retaining screws, cut the upper crossbar out with a hacksaw, and protect the stubs with black gloss paint – it's as simple as that. If you should obtain a stubborn one, be careful if you have to cut out the crossbar on the 6500c to obtain enough leeway to insert the new bar in the vacant holes – you may end up with a warped frame.

For maximum efficiency you should lay the line on a multiplier evenly by hand for the first 45 m (50 yd) of line, with each of the coils touching. This provides a good base for the following line, which is laid fairly even by the side-to-side motion of your thumb on the retrieve. Laying the line on in this way increases capacity and helps an even flow of line through the cast. It also helps to balance the spool. Fill to within one-eighth of the spool lip, and then add your leader.

Fixed spools are notoriously bad for their poor line lay and need attention before fishing. The best way is to fill the spool with about a half of its true capacity, and to look how the line is laid. If the line has built up at the two ends with a hollow in the middle, you remove all the line and refill by hand, but this time build a high point at the middle with less line at each

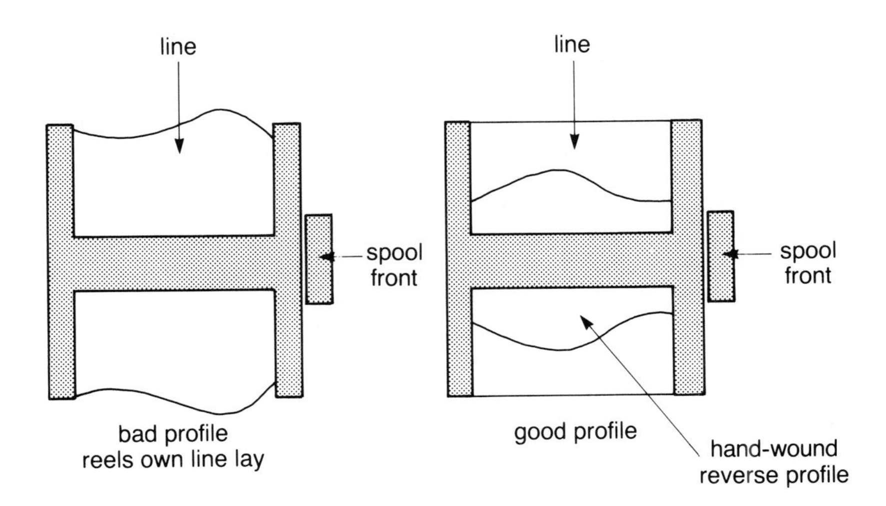

Fig. 32
Fixed-spool reel, line profile

end. When about half a spool is full, click the bale arm in and wind on as normal. This should give you a fairly level line or slightly cone-shaped profile (see Fig. 32). It's critical to fill the spool right to the lip to reduce friction as the line spills over the spool rim. On metal spools it does no harm to polish the rim with metal polish to minimise resistance.

Good models are available from the companies already mentioned, but Daiwa's ST800D, with the tapered spool, has a particularly good line lay and excellent casting performance, coupled with an ideal line capacity at 235 m (260 yd) of 6.8–7.3-kg (15-lb) test. Many other models have line capacities far exceeding this, which is unnecessary.

LINES

Most brands of line have been around for a good few years, and though price is a good guide to quality it's not infallible. If your casting is reliable and you fish clean beaches, there's nothing to stop you using some of the more expensive, but better-quality, lines such as Berkeley Trylene or Stren. However, for over rougher ground go for a middle-priced line such as Maxima, Sylcast, or ABU test – all these are reliable. If the going gets really tough, some of the cheaper ones come into their own – but buy a slightly higher test strength than you would normally, to allow for any variation in reliability.

Always fish as light as conditions allow, for you'll then achieve more bites and enjoy the fish you hook far more. Also, the slimmer the diameter of the line used, the less lead it takes to hold bottom, and the greater the detail of bite indication.

LEADERS

Over rough ground I never use a leader when fishing alone, but for any casting action where other anglers or people are in your vicinity, you'd be an inconsiderate fool not to. Always use a leader at least ten times in grammes/pounds the weight of your sinker: in other words, 30 g = 300 g, 60 g = 600 g, 90 g = 900 g (1 oz = 10 oz, 2 oz = 20 oz, 3 oz = 30 oz), and so on. This gives a fair ammount of safety. Use a soft mono-filament for leaders as this leaves the spool in gentle coils and doesn't fly up on itself. The length is very important: it's rarely advisable to use leaders longer than 7.5 m (25 ft) on standard surf rods, as it's essential to have the leader off the spool before the spool hits full speed. Longer leaders are sometimes advised where heavy fish have to be manhandled near rock faces or steep drop-offs, but casting with leaders longer than 9 m (30 ft) can cause problems. I've included a leader knot diagram (Fig. 33) which is the only one I use, having great faith in its strength and reliability. It's also easy to tie on a wind-swept beach in the middle of winter.

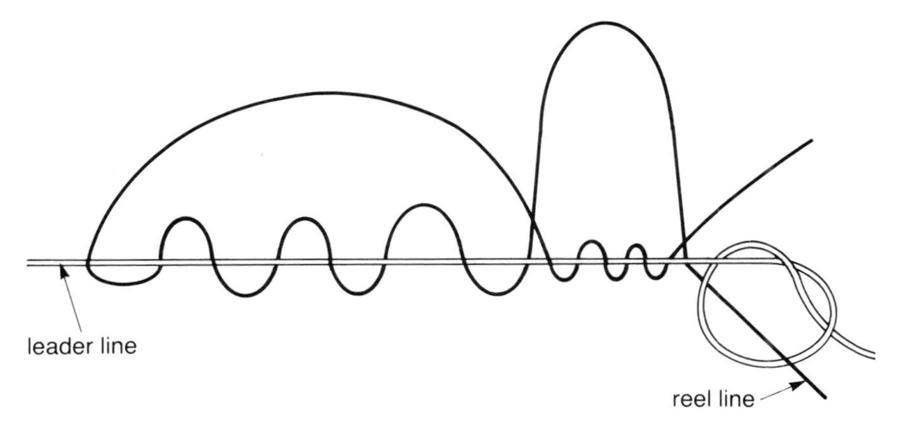

Fig. 33
Leader knot

SWIVELS

Most people use far too big a swivel when casting only a few metres, so keep them small when close up over snaggy ground. You'll lose less this way, but when casting hard and far, a large swivel is good insurance against the added strain – at least it's on top of the job. Beware of cheap swivels that pull apart with little more than finger pressure. After each session, rinse your swivels in freshwater, rechecking their condition before re-using them. If there is any corrosion it's best to throw them away and start again. You can drop them in a little pilchard oil after washing and drying them – this keeps them in good condition a little longer. Over rough ground, split rings in their smaller sizes are often used, but I prefer swivels as the line can catch in the entry and exit of the split ring, and so fray – I won't take the risk.

HOOKS

Hooks need careful selection. There are plenty of patterns about, but few really stand up to the task in hand. What do we look for in a good hook? Take a look at a bass's mouth for a start: it's relatively large in proportion to the size of the fish, and is fairly bony except around the scissors. Hooks made from thick gauge wire are of no use, for they are the hardest to bury past the barb. The wire should be slim, but strong enough to cope with holding fish over the terrain you are to fish. Long-range work, out past the 90-m (100-yd) band requires a short point and small barbs, for at this distance you're relying to a great extent on the fish hooking itself, or at least semi-burying the point in its lip. It's then up to you to make sure the barb goes in by taking up the slack in the line and holding a steady pressure.

For worm baits out at range, I'd go for a 2/0 to 4/0 Aberdeen – but go up to 6/0 or even 7/0 for a crab bait. One point is worth mentioning about long-shanked hooks, however. If you're likely to hook big fish consistently over shallow sand, the perpetual loss of fish halfway through the fight could be caused by leverage – the result of having a good portion of the hook shank protruding from the fish's mouth, which, on contact with the lip, exerts an outward pressure on the hook hold. A change to a shorter-shanked hook would be advisable – any leverage caused by line and lip pressure is forward, encouraging a firmer hook hold.

Deep water and fast tides dictate the use of strong hooks, with strong wire, for not only will the fish hooked exert its own swimming volition but you will also have to contend with that of the tide. The nature of the mark you are fishing will mean that this heavy pull is likely to be at an acute angle, putting massive pressure on the bend of the hook shank. Small points and barbs are still worth having, but hook-ups are usually less of a problem because of the steep angle of the line, which encourages easy sinking past the barb.

Over rough ground is it better to use a long or a short shank? I'm of the opinion that it doesn't matter a great deal, though I usually go for a long shank that presents a good helping of crab meat right up the shank, yet leaving the point well clear. The size is again 6/0 or 7/0, though 4/0 to 6/0 will do in a short shank. The following is a short list of hooks that currently find a home in my tackle box at some point in the bassing season. A Mustad Aberdeen 3282, an ideal crab hook in size 7/0. It's strong, not too large in the point and barb, and although a nickel finish would be better if it were available in a bronzed version, it's still useful for large launce and some deadbaits. A Mustad Viking 79515, another excellent crab hook, though shorter-shanked than the Aberdeen. It has a bronze finish, but the point and barb size are inconsistent though these can be improved at home. It has useful sizes of 2/0 to 6/0 and a medium-weight wire. A Partridge Z10 Aberdeen, an excellent hook for worm and small crab baits. It has sizes up to 4/0, and is good long range over sand because of its small point and barb. A Partridge Z5 Flashpoint, with sizes up to 7/0, and with smaller sizes for good work at range with worm baits. The larger sizes are useful for crabs. It has a bronze finish with a turned-down eye, and is fairly strong. A Partridge MW John Holden, excellent in sizes 4/0 and 6/0 for crab and worm baits. It has good penetration at long range, yet is still strong. There are other hooks, some of them quite good, but the patterns I've listed cover the majority of my bassing trips for bigger fish.

If you want some sport with schoolies, either choose a smaller size from the patterns listed above or go for a Mustad Aberdeen blue in size 1 or 1/0. These are very sharp, with smallish eyes. They do the least damage to the fish that are to be returned, and should you leave the hook in one, through a snap-out, it will rot quickly.

Hooks are never sharp enough straight out of the box, so it's always best to give them a rub with a stone before and during the session to keep them at their most effective. For right-handed anglers, it's best to hold the hook in your left hand with the point facing away from you. The stone is held at 45° to the point, facing in towards the shank. Lubricate the stone with saliva or water, and use an equal amount of strokes either side towards the point. This slims the point down and creates a cutting edge on its inside.

Take any burr off the point itself with a gentle stroke or two, and you should have an ultra-needle-sharp hook. Don't thin the point too much or the strength will be impaired. Any contact with bone may break the point, and the fish will be lost.

The barbs on many hooks are too large, and it's sensible to indulge in a little modification either with the stone (by reducing the actual size of the barb) or with pliers (by breaking a piece off). I'm not in favour of removing barbs altogether, as bass often give slack-line bites and some insurance is often appreciated, especially over the rocks. The best stones for hooks are lathe-slip stones, triangular in shape. They're very tough and last for years. Standard Indian carborundum-type stones in small sizes are fine, though they don't last too long. A piece of 120 or 180 wet-and-dry sandpaper is good for the finer sizes of blued Aberdeens.

There's no need to throw away the hooks you used last session if they're still sound. Giving them a quick wash in warm water when you return home keeps them in the pink. It's the wear and tear on the point that dictates the hook's longevity. Avoid rusty shanks and barbs.

LEADS

For long-range fishing, a long-tailed lead is best, as the tail acts like a dart flight, giving added stability through the cast and increasing casting distance by a few metres. On sand, with the addition of grip leads, anchorage is improved because the tail pulls the wires deeper. A torpedo or sharp-pear shape is the best, as this cuts the air when travelling. Standard, short-loop pear-shaped leads are good for letting the bait trot down sand banks and so on. Spiral leads are useful if you need to troll deep, and sizes in all varieties are handy between 28 and 225 g (1 and 8 oz). If you need more than 225 g (8 oz) to hold bottom, bass are unlikely to be present in any numbers. You can often get away with 170 g (6 oz) when everybody else has to employ 225 g (8 oz) by putting two sinkers together as in Fig. 34. This spreads adhesion and yet still casts reasonably well.

Always use a strong link or split ring to attach your lead to the line, as on the retrieve abrasion from sand and pebbles will soon wear through the knot when the lead is dragged backwards. The addition of the link keeps the knot off the sand. I use only Mustad Oval split rings for this, and need not consider any others. They are just right in size 3/0. Besides, we don't want 170 g (6-oz) weights skipping across crowded beaches.

It pays, in the long run, to make your own leads, especially the release types. These are expensive when losses are high. Don't make the mistake of carrying ready-wired leads in your bag – it's better to pre-cut the wire lengths and make up your spiked leads on the beach, with the wires through the holes in the nose of the lead. I prefer to use elastic bands to tension the wires. Beads are less effective. A few leads with static nose wires are useful for the worst conditions, but if needed you're probably better off at home.

I can't prove it makes any difference, but I won't use a freshly melted lead when after bass. I either use an already well-battered lead, or soak new ones

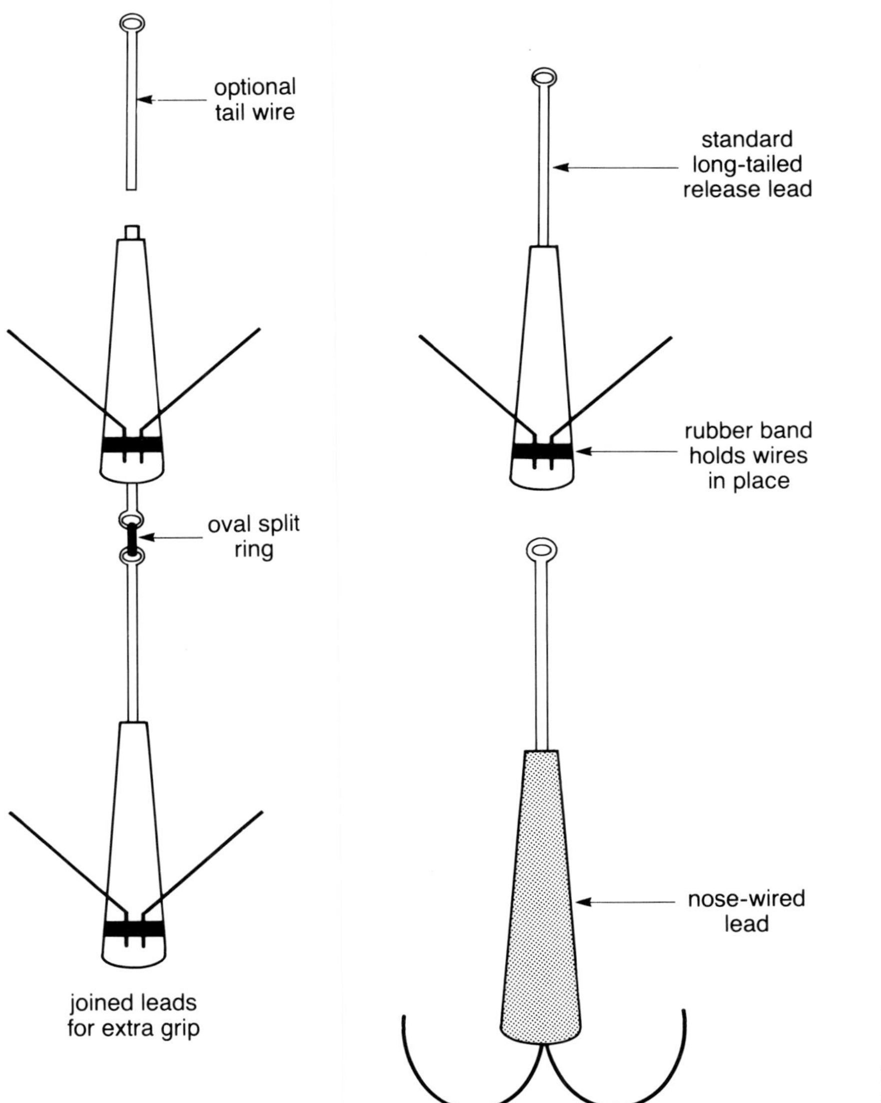

Fig. 34
Wired leads

in vinegar and Yorkshire relish. This dulls the lead and avoids spooking the fish through reflection.

OTHER EQUIPMENT

The choice of terminal tackle and rig on the day is often the dividing line between success and failure. I'm not one of those who believe that a couple of centimetres extra in the length of the trace is going to make any difference. However, it's vitally important to consider how the bait will move. The rig we use may be good for bite indication, without alarming the fish through excessive resistance, but on occasion is resistance really a desirable ally?

Over snaggy ground, with no more than a moderate depth, I use a running ledger. This is a small swivel tied directly to the main line, with a free-running one attached only by one eye above it. To the attached swivel I tie a hook trace of 23 or 25 cm (9 or 10 in) maximum, whilst to the free-running swivel I tie 0.5–0.8 (2–2½ ft) of weaker line, to which the lead or spark plug or whatever other expendable weight will be fastened. The short-hook length gives immediate notification that a bass is interested, and offers the bait naturally without letting the whole affair bounce around uncontrollably. The long-lead link means even a small weight will lead a large bait out on the cast, and the further the hook link is from the lead, the better the bite indication becomes. A weaker line to hook and weight means an easy snap-out if either become jammed in the rocks. Swivels are rarely lost if they are kept small (see Fig. 35).

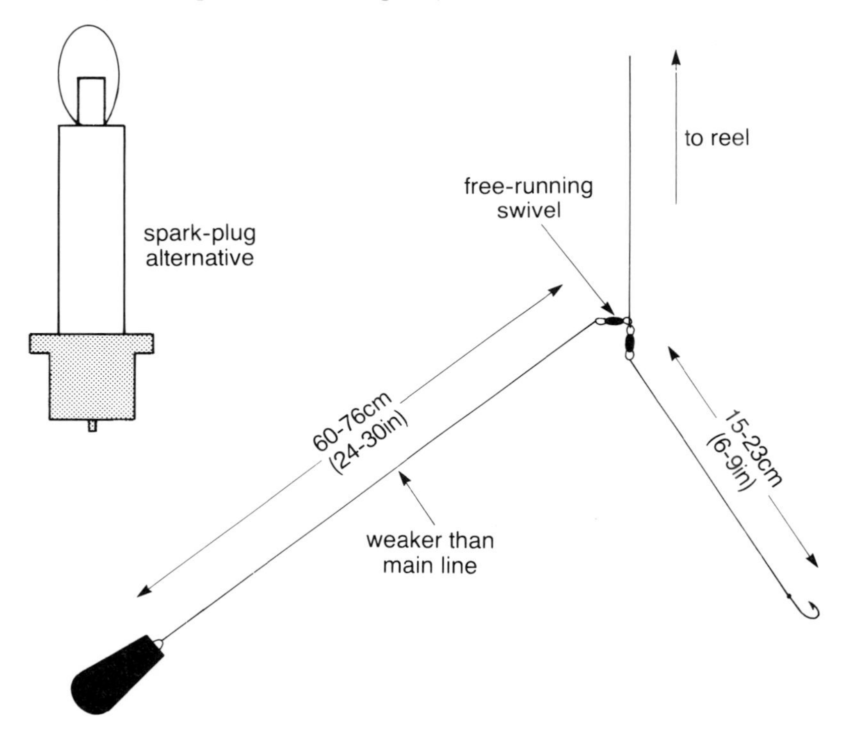

Fig. 35
Running paternoster for rough ground

For deeper water, with a fast tide run – whether over a rough bottom or sand – for down the sides of estuary channels and creeks, for sand banks within easy casting range, and for most boat work, I'd go for the running ledger with a long, flowing trace. There are a couple of ways to construct this, but for estuaries and sand banks I'd use the following: a swivel tied directly, and one to run free as before, only this time the short link – say,

30 cm (1 ft) – goes on the free swivel; to this you tie your lead, whilst the attached swivel holds the hook length 1–2 m (3–6 ft). This will cast moderately well, but makes the bait flutter in the tide. It's a good way of presenting sand-eels (see Fig. 36).

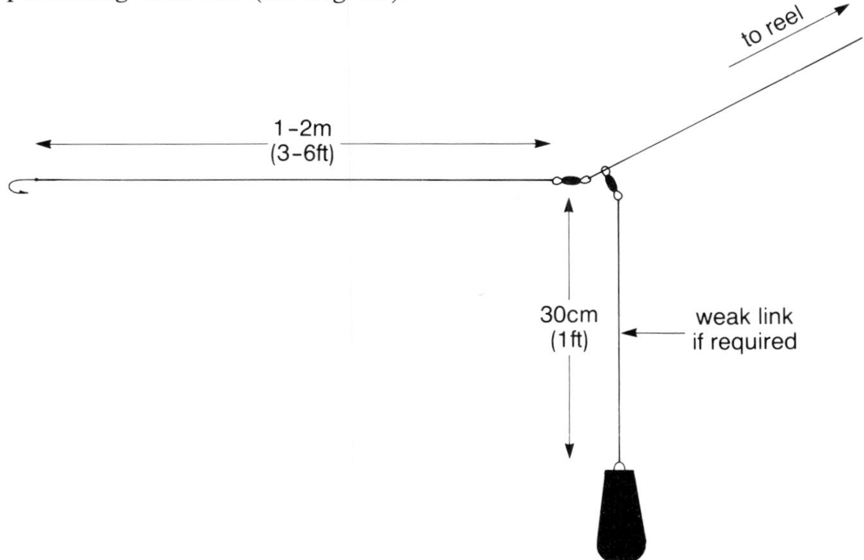

Fig. 36
Running ledger for casting into fast water on rough ground

The second method of construction is for deep water and boat marks. A snap-link swivel or zip slider is fed up the line, followed by a large bead and a swivel, which is tied by one eye. The hook trace – as long as you wish it – can be added to the free end. The running link holds the lead, though if the bottom is bad you can add 8 or 10 cm (3 or 4 in) of weak line so that you only lose your weight. A further variation is to lengthen the lead link so that, if the rod is held and the line kept tight, the bait will flutter just off the bottom (see Fig. 37).

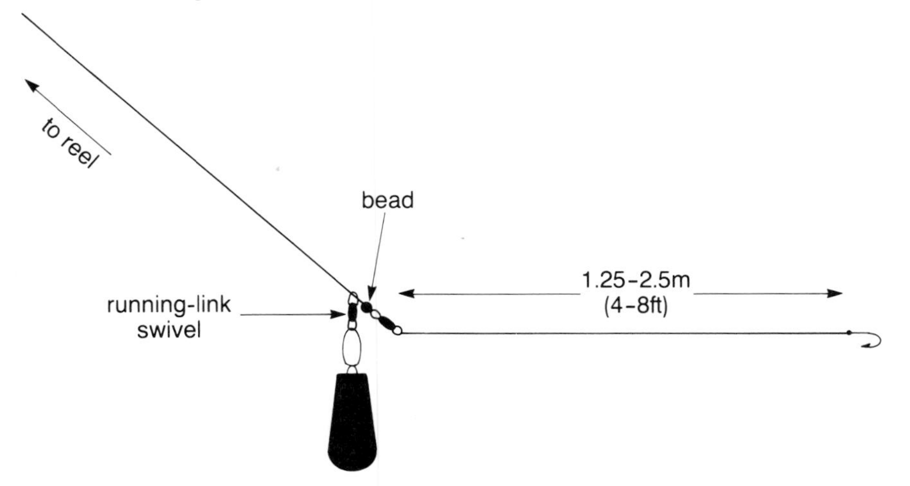

Fig. 37
Running trace for boat work

For all surf work and long-range casting, I use the fixed paternoster, which is simple to construct. Take a piece of line about 0.8 m (30 in) long, which is capable of casting the weight you intend to use. Tie a 3/0 oval split ring to the base, then from the top slide on a piece of PVC tubing (taken from electricians's wire) that is a reasonable match to the diameter of the line. This is then super-glued in the correct place. Follow this with a small bead and free-running swivel, then another bead and further length of PVC

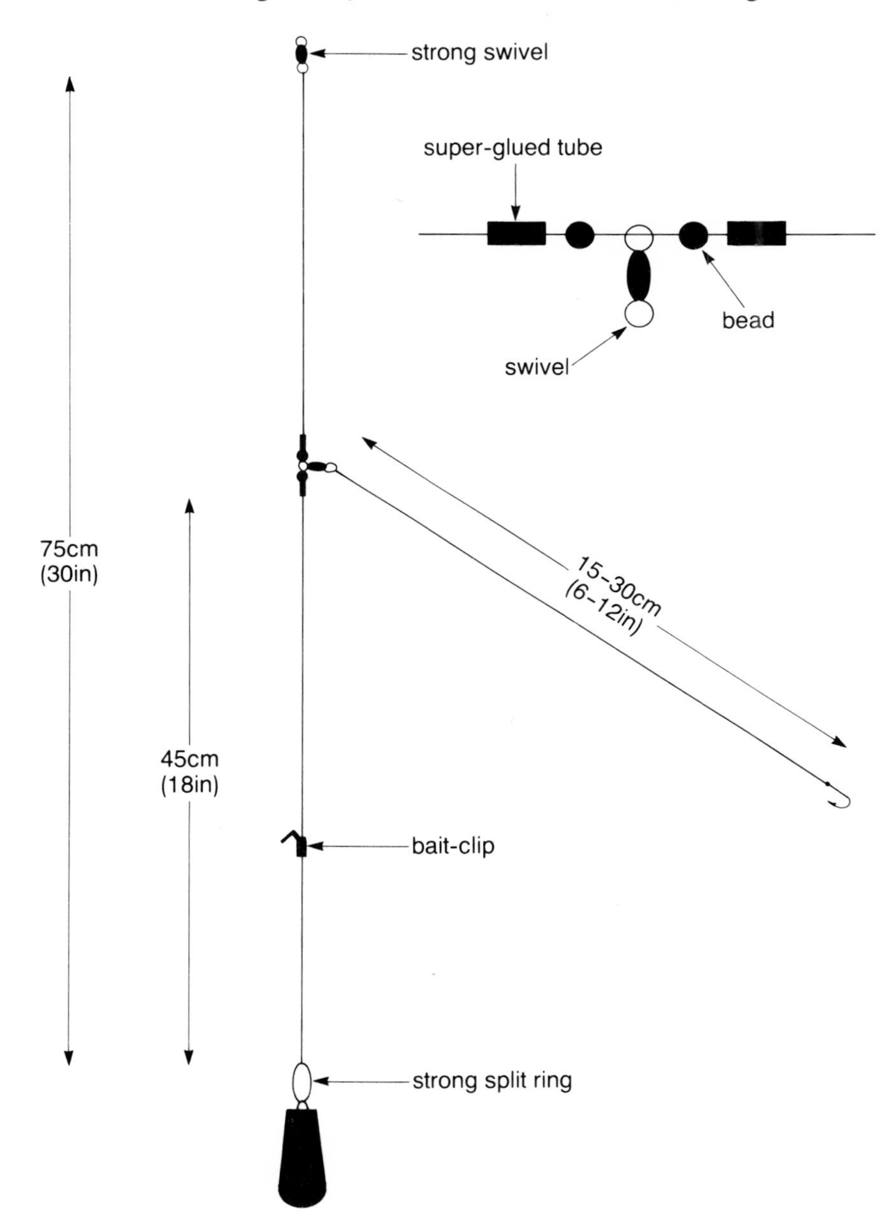

Fig. 38
Fixed paternoster – distance-casting rig

tubing (again super-glued). Leave enough room between the tubing for the beads and swivel to turn freely. You can dispense with the tube, and super-glue the bead if you prefer (see Fig. 38).

Hook lengths tied to the spinning swivel can be 15–30 cm (6–12 in), with the distance from the bead to the swivel not less than 45 cm (18 in). Bait-clips (either home-made from electrician's wire and tubing) or commercial ones hold the hook in place during the cast, which presents the bait better. For casts under 73 m (80 yd), it's best to dispense with the clip as release problems occur (see Fig. 39).

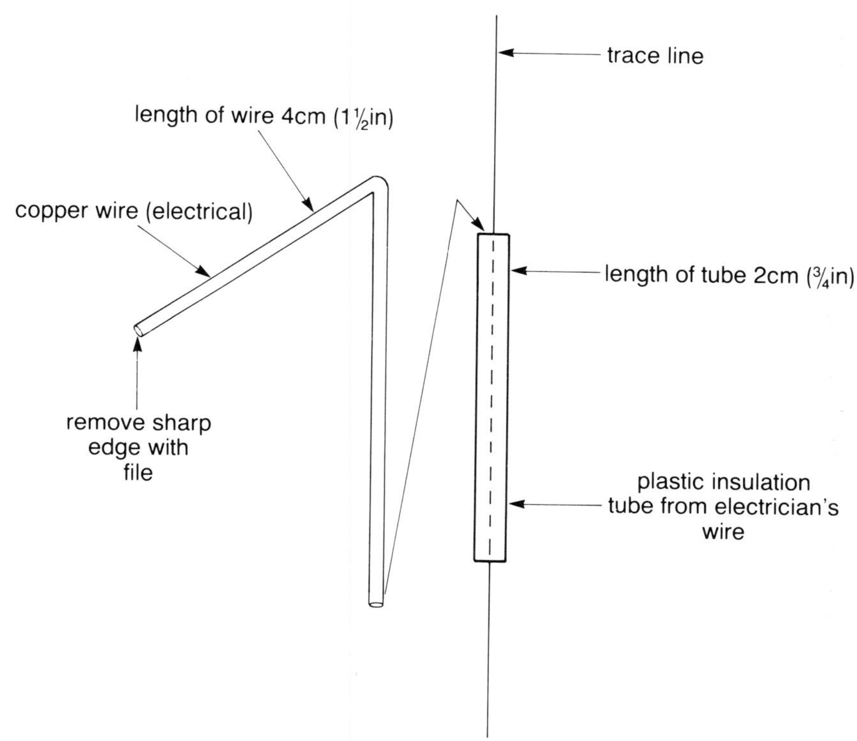

Fig. 39 Home-made bait-clip

It's rare for the glued beads or tubing to slip, but if they do – even with a fish on – it's not of any consequence, so don't spend time worrying. Slight variations on the trace length are worth considering: a long one, clipping the bait directly behind the lead, gives excellent distance as the bait flies in the broken air, caused by the passage of the lead. The long trace gives plenty of movement and so plenty of time for finicky fish to accept the offering. Traces as long as 2–2.5 m (6–8 ft) can be cast when using pendulum styles, and whilst examples are rare it's worth giving them a try when bites are scarce. Simply increase the distance between the beads and the lead to that required.

For close-quarter situations, where bass of decent size may hit hard and run, placing the bead-trapped swivel 15 cm (6 in) above the lead takes away the natural softening effect of the line, causing the fish to come up hard

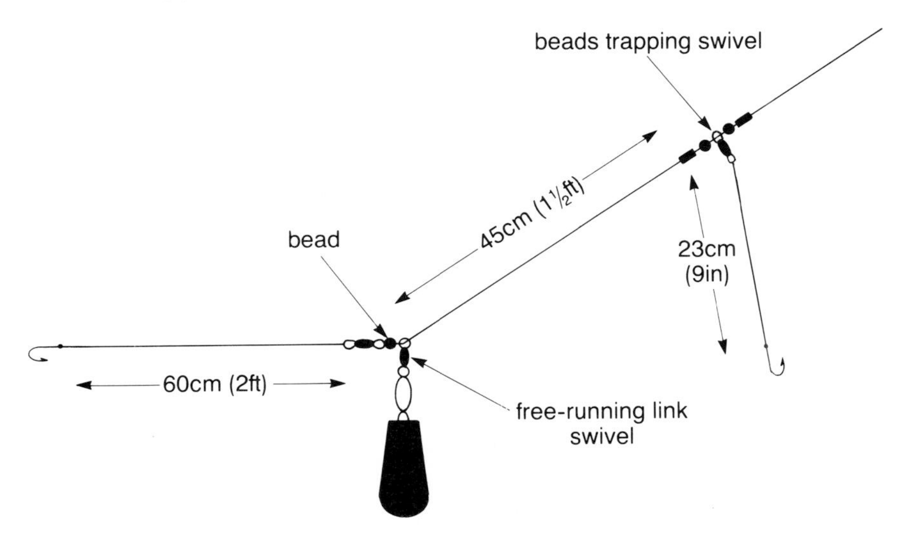

Fig. 40
Two-hook rig

against the lead and so hooking itself in the process. Two hook rigs for bass are not acceptable to me, but for those who feel more confident with two hooks, the best rig is a mixture of a fixed and running paternoster. Basically, make the top half of the trace with beads as normal, but instead of the split ring you first slide on a snap link and swivel. Then a bead is followed by a largish swivel. To this you tie a longish trace, with a short one as normal on the upper trapped swivel. The lead goes on the snap link (see Fig. 40).

A two-hook spreader is worth using when you fish for schoolies. Use two bead-trapped swivels spaced 45 cm (18 in) apart. Try crab on the upper hook and worm on the lower, and swap them round until you find what and where the fish want it. I prefer using one hook and fishing light for sport (see Fig. 41).

When trolling from a boat, if you need extra depth the only lead worth considering is the spiral lead, which can be wound on the line after tackle assembly. The beauty of these is that you can alter them instantly up or down for extra movement in the trace.

Float gear is simple. Slide the line through the tube or eyes of the float, and then a drilled bullet large enough to cock the float. Stop this with a swivel and a bead, and attach your hook length. To set the float at a pre-decided depth, I use a piece of elastic band. Choose cylindrical floats that offer less resistance to the taking fish. Avoid the top-heavy pike-bungs that are too buoyant for easy submersion. The choice of colour is usually vivid, but on water black is the colour most often easily seen against light reflection. Otherwise, yellow and white are fine (see Fig. 42).

A couple of clear-plastic bubble floats are useful if you need to cast a little further. You can can rough them up with a little wet-and-dry sandpaper and repaint them the colour you prefer. These are ideal when using a longish trace with nothing more attached than a hook and bait. The longer the trace you can manage, so much the better: the float follows the current

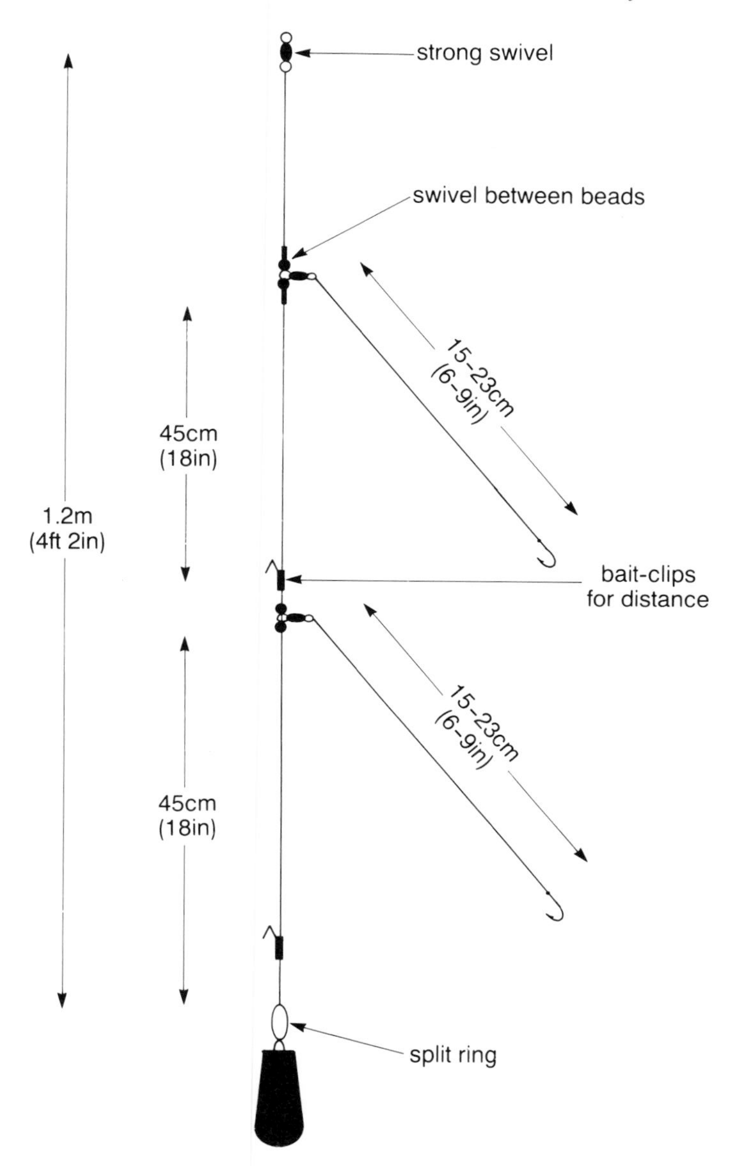

Fig. 41
Two-hook spreader

and the bait bounces and bumps its way downtide – a very natural presentation.

Don't be static in your choice of trace line: think about it. In rough weather, when the sea is coloured, a 35-kg (80-lb) trace wouldn't put a bass off, but in calm clear conditions they become gut shy and often veer away. I noticed that bites dropped off as the water shallowed and cleared, and for a while I accepted this as fact. But then I began to experiment with lighter lines and longer traces in periods of calm, clear conditions. Straight away

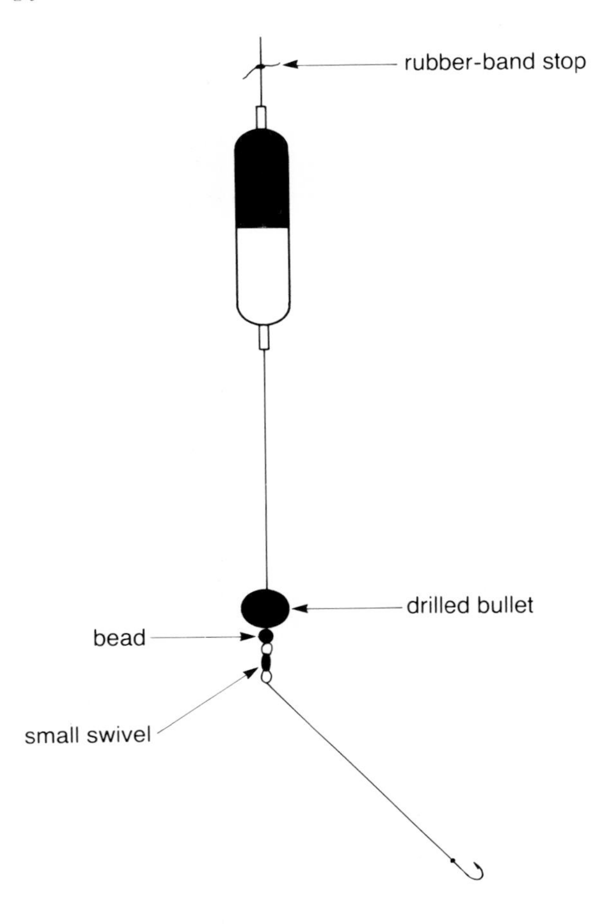

Fig. 42
Float tackle

my results improved. Obviously, the governing factor is the terrain over which you cast, but over sand I've used 2.75-kg (6-lb) traces with 3.6–4.5-kg (8–10-lb) main line, and very small swivels with no beads – just knots to keep the swivel in place. What had formerly been shy, almost ghostly bites, now pulled the rod tip hard over.

Whether the colour of the line puts the fish off or attracts them is a difficult question. Again, I try to avoid heavy leaders that contrast starkly with the background, although one thing I haven't tried is whether flourescent lines used in coloured water actually attract bass. Clear monolines are the best for traces on calm days, for obvious reasons. Brown lines would seem safe for rocky bottoms. These little things just give you the edge.

You'll need a good headlight, though even the cheap ones are serviceable if strengthened with a little extra solder on the connections, and 0.6 m (2 ft) of extra wire are spliced into the middle of the lead to allow freedom during casting. Whichever make you buy, make sure the size of batteries it requires are available as rechargable units. Even someone who fishes three or four times a week will find these batteries last three seasons, and the charger will soldier on for years. The savings can be measured in hundreds of pounds. Incidentally, by making sure you use all the power in a set of batteries before you recharge them will make them last even longer. Tape a spare bulb to the lamp frame in case of emergencies.

For those of us who need to keep our marks under wraps, the light from our headlamps needs to be restricted, yet sufficient to give us enough light to work by. Cut the shape of your lamp lens out of a child's sun visor, either of blue or red plastic, and tape this over the top. You'll have enough light to fish by, but the intense beam seen anything up to a mile or so away is reduced. Only use pressure lamps as a last resort – they attract humans as well as moths.

Always carry a pair of small long-nosed pliers – they're far more adept at removing hooks from fish's jaws than your fingers, and are handy for other fishing chores as well. If you must take a tacklebag with you, a small waterproof rucksack is ideal, as all your gear is on your back leaving your hands free. If you intend to use a landing-net on a rock mark or two, look around for one carp catchers use – they are roomy and give a big target when working in low-light levels. Triangular nets are adequate but if possible I prefer a round shape. Carp nets are more sturdily built than most commercial versions, but there's no point in going overboard by purchasing a huge one designed to take a record carp – it's you who's got to carry it.

Very few knots are needed. I really only use two for tackle assembly, but I've included a diagram of the tucked half-blood knot which is good for attaching hooks and swivels, as is the uni-knot (see Fig. 43). A simple paternoster loop can be formed as in Fig. 44, doing away with the bead and swivel. However, if you use the trace complete with blood loop for several sessions, the blood loop will tighten and may snap on the cast. Use it once, then make a fresh trace. Other knots may suggest themselves from time to time, but always run the untightened knot through your mouth so the saliva acts as a lubricant on the line, when the knot is tightened. This avoids friction burn and encourages a close neat knot. When over rough ground, or when hitting the cast hard check all knots frequently from the leader knot down.

Having something upon which to rest your rod, during rebaiting keeps the worst of the sand and rubbish off your gear. On sand, a simple monopod is easily made from a 1-m (3-ft) length of 10-mm ($\frac{3}{8}$-in) steel rod

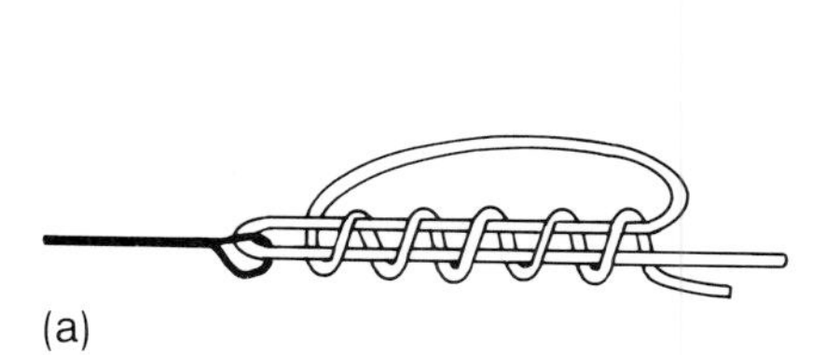

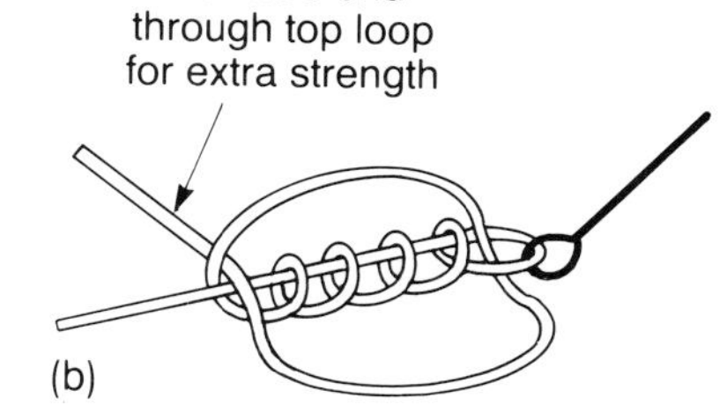

Fig. 43
Knots to attach hooks and swivels: (a) uni-knot; (b) tucked half-blood knot

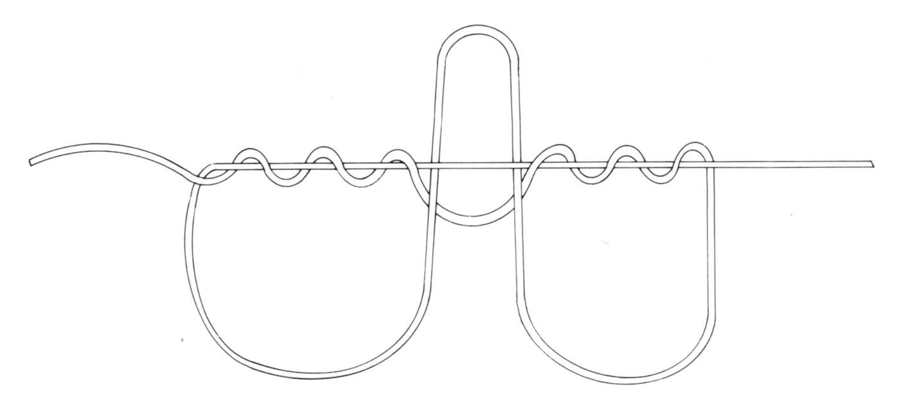

Fig. 44
Blood loop

slightly sharpened at one end and with a small, flat plate welded 15 cm (6 in), up from this to stop twisting when the rod is pulling into the tide. From the sharp end, 45 cm (18 in) up, weld a piece of exhaust tubing, say, 8 cm (3 in) long with an inside diameter of 5 cm (2 in), into which the rod butt is placed. Finally, a length of rod or bar, bent to the shape of a V or U, takes the upper part of the butt. The distance between the cup and the top should be such that your reel is just above the U or V-shape when the rod is in position. If you can obtain it, the same length in triangulated stainless steel is strong, light, and won't rust.

Rough ground and shingle beaches dictate the use of a tripod, either of metal or wood. The construction of one of these is simple, but always, when fishing with the rod or rods in the tripod, weigh it down with a bag of beach pebble suspended from the middle, or stack large pebbles around its legs – these tripods are prone to collapsing when weed, a fish, or just the wind catches it in the right place.

CASTING

Having already mentioned a few casting styles, it occurred to me that some beginners might be confused. It may, therefore, be worthwhile describing very quickly the different styles of casting. However, while reading about casting can be helpful, the beginner ultimately needs practical guidance from an experienced tutor.

The overhead thump is exactly that – the rod tip is swung away from the sea to face in the opposite direction, with the lead hanging around 1 m (3 ft) from the tip. The forward movement is round and up, with the right arm (for right-handed people) punching skywards. The left hand is lazy during this cast, and acts more like a pivot than anything else. This type of cast is all arm action. A much more effective way is to lay the sinker on the floor and, with the arms out and more or less straight from the chest (which faces to your original right when facing the sea), the lead is pulled from the floor and hurled skyward, by the rising arc and push of the right hand, coupled with the upward, then downward, pull of the left. Extra power comes from lengthening the drop of line to the lead by 2–2.5 m (6–8 ft) and increasing the arc of the rod by forcing the upper part of your body further round, away from the sea. This is called 'off the ground'. You're beginning to use your body's back and leg muscles as well as your arms, which vastly increases power.

The pendulum is the most versatile and powerful cast. It is basically the same as off the ground, and although you use the same body movements and arc, you now swing the sinker on a long drop of 2.5 or 2.7 m (8 or 9 ft) away from you, the rod being held amost vertically in front of your face. This outward motion of the lead is created by pushing out with your right hand. When the sinker peaks on its furthest travel, you then reverse this by punching down with your left hand. The sinker now climbs high above your head. When it peaks, this cast is very much like the movements used in the off the ground.

Please note this is a vast over-simplification, purely to help beginners recognise which styles are which, and to put a name to them. It's up to them to find the information and teaching that's available, the versatility and greater enjoyment available to those willing to learn is great. Bass are often caught close in, but not always. To have the ability to drop a good-sized bait on the edge of a rough patch 120 m (130 yd) or more from dry sand is an asset at least equal to any financial one. The more skills you acquire, the greater the catch on the night.

11 Conservation

If it wasn't for humanity's rapid technological advances there would be no need for conservation. Fishing methods employed even up to the beginning of the last war were primitive. To a great extent they were ineffective, allowing the majority of the fish to escape, thus keeping breeding stocks constant and inshore catches consistent. With the last war came radar and depth sounders. For the first time humanity began to see a picture of the sea bed underneath its craft. Fish finders were quick to follow. The old skills of knowing where the shoals would be at particular times of the year ceased to be of importance. Huge trawlers swept the sea bed devoid of life, taking what was previously a year's catch in just a few weeks. Famous old fishing grounds, such as the Dogger Bank, slowly began to produce fewer fish, which meant that larger boats began to work further and further afield until those grounds in turn were fished almost dry. Vast trawler fleets began to dwindle, but catches remained high because of humanity's mechanical and technical ability. A great British industry was stifled by greed.

Whilst all this was going on, bass to a certain degree were safe from major commercial activity. Bass had received little by way of study, and so its habits and environment remained a mystery to the majority. Only isolated bass showed up in inshore long-line catches. The nearest thing to modern-day slaughter was when the small boats of Cornwall and Wales were launched to net huge shoals of bass feeding on small baitfish. Even then many escaped.

Rod and line results, by comparison, have always been of little consequence. Occasionally bass can be suicidal and hit anything you throw at them, though these occasions are few and far between. By the very nature of the tackle we use which is slow and selective, overall damage is minimal – though not to be ignored.

The tide turned away from bass with the coming of the nylon monofilament gill net. These festoon wrecks and are strategically placed around reef systems, such as the Manacles and Eddystone, where bass are likely to shoal for breeding and feeding. Set across the low-tide mark of rough-ground beaches, across the bars of estuaries, this has become a nationwide problem. The areas worst affected are North Wales, between the tip of the Lleyn peninsula and Anglesey, and also parts of South Wales and Devon and Cornwall. If you stand on high cliffs, the extent of the gill netters work can be seen. Placed in such numbers and in such a manner, it's hard to imagine how bass ever find their way inshore.

During storms, the nets set around reefs and wrecks break free and become attached to the rocks and superstructure. Though these are lost the fishermen, these ghost nets carry on catching fish, one assumes, for years to come. Even onshore I've come across nets that are filled with weed, holding many bass and mullet, and that sit there for weeks on end, tainting the shore with the stench of waste.

It was inevitable, with the increase in bass landings, that the public slowly became aware of the value of this fish's flesh. Restaurants and pubs began to offer encouraging sums to anglers wishing to make a return on their sport – though with the acceptance of money I would have thought that the sporting side would evaporate. Scuba divers got in on the act, spearing fish mainly for sale, and with the recession of the late 1970s and early 1980s many individuals bought small gill nets to set off the shore to supplement their incomes. These nets – set mainly for salmon and seatrout – delighted their owners when numbers of bass also showed up.

As the price of bass per kilogramme rose, so did the efforts to catch them. Caution was thrown to the wind. Some individuals set about long-lining for bass from the shore, using short lengths of mono-line and spade-end commercial whiting hooks. These are left in place for many weeks and visited at each low water for the fish to be collected and the hooks rebaited. This method is called 'spiltering', with bass that are to some extent territorial. These lines consist of around 150 to 200 hooks. You can appreciate that an area's population could be drastically reduced or annihilated completely.

We anglers don't carry halos either. The 'great hunter' photos, with several bass at our feet, are far too common on the mantlepiece or on top of the television. Tourist anglers do untold damage catching and killing small school bass in large numbers. These people know nothing of size limits and protective measures – fish for the pot is what matters. In July and August, any pier or jetty breakwater or groyne holds its population of stiff, dried-out schoolie corpses, a legacy of the throw-away society.

In the 1980s other factors became evident – and all were humanity-induced. Many farms now use chemical fertilisers, which are washed from the land into the streams that feed our estuaries – the native home of bass before adulthood. These nitrates and phosphates encourage new weed growth, the expanding root systems of which hold sand that becomes a permanent bank with the passage of time. Our estuaries are silting up. Financial syndicates appear like mushrooms, intent on turning salt marshes and inlets into vast marinas, destroying valuable nursery sites and altering the natural flow of the estuary's cycle. Whilst the yachts are in harbour, anti-fouling paint flakes off their hulls, and on falling to the sea bed kills the natural fauna, breaking millions-of-years-old links in the natural food chain. The chemical industry adds its waste to our rivers and canals. All this toxicity must eventually find its way to the sea to do its share of the killing.

Whilst acknowledging that the total population of bass has been reduced quite considerably over the twenty-five years of my interest in the sport, things haven't yet become irreparable. There are still a few bass in

1.4-kg (3-lb) bass on a redgill – this fish was returned

existence that offer a useful base for rebuilding and securing the bass stocks of the future.

Of prime consideration is a more practical size limit set by the government. Present limits are far too low. A minimum size of 45 cm (18 in) should be enforced immediately. This national size limit applies to any individual wishing to kill fish, and would – if heavy fines were implemented – do much to protect the juvenile stocks. These young fish are relatively easy to catch in large numbers, and it's here that the damage is done to future breeding generations. By protecting the hordes of juveniles until they've had adequate time to spawn means greater numbers of these small fish will have the opportunity to grow, giving a higher population of bigger, fully mature individuals.

For far too long in the angling world, there's been a 'holier than thou' attitude that is far from the truth. Anglers seeking the respect of their compatriots return very large fish. While agreeing this is most admirable the incidences of these large fish – within the bounds of common sense – are few and far between. Few anglers have the temperament and dedication it takes to catch bass over 1.8 or 2.3 kg (4 or 5 lb) on a regular basis, and by taking a few fish for the table you're not going to put the species at risk, providing every fish under your own size limit goes back. I have a permanent limit of 1.4 kg (3 lb) but rarely kill fish under 1.8 or 2.3 kg (4 or 5 lb). By conforming to this, a successful angler should have a return ratio of around 70 per cent, with less successful individuals having a ratio of better than 90 per cent.

Of course, that's in an ideal world where everybody is honest. Apart from those who do disregard the size limit by returning all fish under 45 cm (18 in), a return factor of about 75 – 80 per cent should be enjoyed by the bass, certainly enough to encourage an increase in numbers. As an angler you have a duty to treat your catch with care and respect to enable it to return to the water unharmed. Small bass are best laid out on the sand, or if you're on rocks, held gently with a wet cloth. Never hold any fish with dry hands. The hook should be gently worked from either side until the barb comes away. Should the hook be buried in the tongue or lower jaw, the least damaging way is to cut the hook trace and pull the point and barb through, and extract the hook by pulling the eye and shank through the hole made by the point and barb. Never poke your fingers deep into the throat of a fish you wish to return. For deep-hooked fish, use long-nosed pliers or cutters, and if the hook is stubborn, cut through the shank and feed the hook out backwards. Again, if the hook refuses to budge at all, cut the shank as short as possible and return the fish with the point still embedded. It will soon rot away and do less damage than your deep delving.

To return fish to the water means walking out into the surf, into a half a metre or more of water. By holding the bass under the tail and just aft of the chin, with the majority of the body being covered by water, they just swim away when ready, often with a speedy rush. Never throw them waterwards by using an under-arm or over-arm action – this is brutal and disgusting. On rock marks, wading is often impractical, so providing the tide is on the flood I prefer to find a pool deep enough to take the fish. The tide floods the pool and I let nature do the rest.

Bass are surprisingly tough and can stand a little rough treatment, but it's good to return them to the water within two minutes. Any fish that floats on its side is in trouble, but by holding its head into a well-oxygenated surf you may be able to rescue the situation. It's very rare for one to expire altogether – I can't remember the last time it happened to me. Take your time, be gentle, don't be afraid to lose a hook, and you won't go far wrong.

There are other forms of protection worth looking at. At the time of writing, there are proposals for closed nursery areas to be designated, probably in estuaries and suitable sections of the coast line. This would seem to be an ideal set-up, but some suggestion has been made to the effect that some commercial fishing may, under licence, be allowed to continue. This is far from satisfactory. A closed area for the protection of juvenile fish should be just that: a closed area to all. When the population for the closed area became too large, it would spill out into the surrounding areas, and have a knock-on effect that would benefit all.

Raising of the minimum mesh size used by netsmen would seem an obvious step, allowing the juvenile fish to swim through but catching large fish as before. This really goes hand-in-hand with the higher minimum size, for if they raise the minimum size but leave the mesh size the same as before, the bass will still be caught and die as a result of the net (though the netsman is legally restricted from bringing this catch home. There will always be a bone of contention between the commercial fisher and the angler because anglers are always told to leave a commercial fisher's buisness and livelihood alone. It's of little consequence that the commercial fishers are killing their own livelihood by over-exploitation of young fish.

Still on a commercial theme, over the past couple of winters foreign trawlers have severely decimated huge shoals of bass in the English Channel. As these fish congregate *en masse* from all sections of the British coast line and from northern European waters the suggested catch tonnage is worrying. If left unchecked this will result in problems. Catch quotas would help to some degree, but would be hard to enforce because of the numerous ways of covering up deals involving the sale of fish, and British boats swapping boxes of fish with foreign trawlers for hard cash.

Public awareness has, as yet been left untouched. The problem is that the people who are most likely to cause problems, such as the tourist who takes a few schoolies off the end of the pier, never reads an angling magazine or publication. Most likely, the tourist doesn't even know a size limit exists, even though these are displayed on most quays and harbour walls. Perhaps they should be displayed on all man-made structures where fishing takes place.

Fish farming is, I admit, something I know little about, but I would assume if it were to be undertaken it would prove very expensive and I have doubts as to its effectiveness. However, because of the bass's more solitary nature, perhaps the procurement of eggs and their encouragement to develop into fingerlings for distribution amongst the nursery grounds could be tried, much as is done with salmon and seatrout. This may induce a better success rate than that provided by nature.

Another point of interest is that many juvenile bass are found dead in the intakes of nuclear power-stations. The outgoing warm water attracts them in the first place. These could be the ideal venues for experimentation with artificial rearing. Having said all this, I would dislike to see a truly wild fish become as domesticated as some of the stewpond trout you see being put into the fishing reservoirs – it's better to protect the bass in its natural environment.

What, then, do we consider the action needed to be? The closed nursery areas should be assessed by identifying those estuaries that are the most prominent existing nursery beds. These should be closed to all. I'm not naive enough to expect that the government impose my 45-cm (18-in) limit, but if a combination of a 38-cm (15-in) minimum landing – size and an increase in the net mesh size to 102 mm (4 in) was enforced, this would help to protect the immature bass in numbers. The present limit of 32 cm (14 in) is unacceptable and should be modified.

It's wrong to assume that the few fish you catch won't make any difference, for you're thinking like the average person. The average person is always in the majority, and that means you're all taking fish. It adds up. Make an effort, and contribute to your sport by controlling your catch with a strict size limit that can be increased when the fishing is good. Besides, the feeling you experience when a big bass flicks its tail, propelling it from your hands out to freedom, is different but equal to any feeling you experience when you return home with a belter to show your friends and family. It does take a form of courage, though, to return and say you released a 2.3-km (5-lb) fish – this usually produces tones of 'pull the other one', but surely your own conscience is all that matters.

Index

Page numbers in *italic* refer to illustrations.